50
Knitted Dolls

50
Knitted Dolls

Sarah Keen

Dedicated to George

First published 2017 by
Guild of Master Craftsman Publications Ltd
Castle Place, 166 High Street, Lewes,
East Sussex, BN7 1XU, UK

Text © Sarah Keen, 2017
Copyright in the Work © GMC Publications Ltd, 2017

ISBN 978 1 78494 346 2

Publisher Jonathan Bailey
Production Manager Jim Bulley
Senior Project Editor Dominique Page
Managing Art Editor Gilda Pacitti
Designer Ginny Zeal
Photographer Andrew Perris
Illustrator Simon Rodway

Set in Frontenac

Colour origination by GMC Reprographics

Printed and bound in Turkey

Contents

Introduction

It's been a happy time for me making these dolls; such a lot of characters all in one book! These cute little makes all measure around 6in (15cm) and can be completed swiftly. They each have individual details without being overly fiddly. You'll find there is something to suit most occasions, and children and adults alike will adore them.

I hope you enjoy making the dolls just as much as I have enjoyed designing them. Happy knitting!

Sarah Keen

The Dolls

Skateboarder

Materials

- ♥ Any DK (US: light worsted) yarn (amounts given are approximate):
  5g royal blue (A)
  5g pale pink (B)
  5g white (C)
  5g deep red (D)
  5g grey (E)
  5g brown (F)
  10g khaki green (G)
  5g black (H)
  5g ginger (I)
- ♥ Oddments of black, red and ginger for embroidery
- ♥ 1 pair of 3.25mm (UK10:US3) needles and a spare needle of the same size
- ♥ Knitters' pins and a blunt-ended needle for sewing up
- ♥ Tweezers (optional)
- ♥ Acrylic toy stuffing
- ♥ A red pencil for shading cheeks
- ♥ Small piece of thick cardboard

Finished size

Skateboarder stands 6in (15cm) tall

Tension

26 sts x 34 rows measure 4in (10cm) square over st-st using 3.25mm needles and DK yarn before stuffing

Abbreviations

See page 219

How to make Skateboarder

SHOES, LEGS, BODY AND HEAD
Right leg
Using the long tail method and A for shoe, cast on 14 sts.
Place a marker on cast-on edge between the 5th and 6th st of the sts just cast on.
Row 1 (WS): Purl.
Row 2: K2, (m1, k2) to end (20 sts).
Rows 3 to 5: Beg with a p row, work 3 rows in st-st.
Row 6: K2, (k2tog) 6 times, k6 (14 sts).
Row 7: P7, p2tog, p1, p2tog, p2 (12 sts).
Rows 8 to 21: Change to B for leg and work 14 rows in st-st.
Break yarn and set aside.

Left leg
Using the long tail method and A for shoe, cast on 14 sts.
Place a marker on cast-on edge between the 9th and 10th st of the sts just cast on.

Row 1 (WS): Purl.
Row 2: K2, (m1, k2) to end (20 sts).
Rows 3 to 5: Beg with a p row, work 3 rows in st-st.
Row 6: K6, (k2tog) 6 times, k2 (14 sts).
Row 7: P2, p2tog, p1, p2tog, p7 (12 sts).
Rows 8 to 21: Change to B for leg and work 14 rows in st-st.

Join legs
Row 22: Change to C for lower body and with RS facing, k across sts of left leg then with the same yarn cont k across sts of right leg (24 sts).
Rows 23 to 27: Beg with a p row, work 5 rows in st-st.
Rows 28 to 37: Change to D for upper body and work 10 rows in st-st.
Rows 38 and 39: Change to B for head and work 2 rows in st-st.
Row 40: K2, (m1, k4) to last 2 sts, m1, k2 (30 sts).

Rows 41 to 49: Beg with a p row, work 9 rows in st-st.
Row 50: (K2tog, k1) to end (20 sts).
Row 51: Purl.
Row 52: (K2tog) to end (10 sts).
Thread yarn through sts on needle and leave loose.

TROUSERS
First leg
Beg at lower edge using the long tail method and E, cast on 21 sts.
Row 1 (RS): Purl.
Rows 2 to 12: Beg with a p row, work 11 rows in st-st.
Rows 13 and 14: Cast off 2 sts at beg of next 2 rows (17 sts).
Break yarn and set aside.

Second leg
Work second leg as for first leg but do not break yarn.

Join legs
Row 15: With RS facing, k across sts of second leg then with the same yarn cont k across sts of first leg (34 sts).
Rows 16 to 20: Beg with a p row, work 5 rows in st-st.
Cast off.

ARMS AND HANDS
(make 2)
Beg at shoulder using the long tail method and B, cast on 4 sts.
Row 1 (WS): Purl.
Row 2: K1, (m1, k1) to end (7 sts).
Row 3: Purl.
Row 4: K1, m1, k to last st, m1, k1 (9 sts).
Rows 5 and 6: Rep rows 3 and 4 once (11 sts).
Rows 7 to 17: Beg with a p row, work 11 rows in st-st.

Front and back
Using the long tail method and G, cast on 38 sts and beg in rib.
Row 1 (WS): (K1, p1) to end.
Row 2: As row 1.
Row 3: Purl.
Join on D and work in stripes, carrying yarn loosely up side of work.
Rows 4 and 5: Using D, work 2 rows in g-st.
Rows 6 and 7: Using G, k 1 row then p 1 row.
Rows 8 to 11: Rep rows 4 to 7 once.
Row 12: Knit.

Divide for armholes
Row 13: P8, cast off 4 sts pwise, p13, cast off 4 sts pwise, p7 (30 sts).

Join sleeves
Row 14: With RS of all pieces facing, k8 from left back, k10 from one sleeve, k14 across front, k10 from other sleeve, k8 from right back (50 sts).
Row 15: P6, (p2tog) twice, p6, (p2tog) twice, p10, (p2tog) twice, p6, (p2tog) twice, p6 (42 sts).
Row 16: K5, (k2tog) twice, k4, (k2tog) twice, k8, (k2tog) twice, k4, (k2tog) twice, k5 (34 sts).

Divide for front opening
Row 17: P15, k4, p15.

Work left back and left front
Row 18: K4, (k2tog) twice, k2, (k2tog) twice, k3, turn and work on these 13 sts.
Row 19: K2, p to end.
Row 20: K4, k2tog, k2, k2tog, k3 (11 sts).
Row 21: As row 19.

Work left side of hood
Row 22: (K2, m1) 4 times, k3 (15 sts).
Row 23: K2, p to end.
Row 24: Knit.
Rows 25 to 46: Rep rows 23 and 24, 11 times more.
Cast off in patt.

Row 18: K2tog, (k1, k2tog) to end (7 sts).
Thread yarn through sts on needle, pull tight and secure by threading yarn a second time through sts.

HAIR
Using the long tail method and F, cast on 30 sts and work in g-st, RS facing to beg.
Rows 1 to 14: Work 14 rows in g-st.
Row 15: (K2tog, k1) to end (20 sts).
Row 16: Knit.
Row 17: (K2tog) to end (10 sts).
Row 18: Knit.
Thread yarn through sts on needle, pull tight and secure by threading yarn a second time through sts.

HOODIE
Note: Sleeves are worked first and knitted into body.

Sleeves (make 2)
Beg at cuff using the long tail method and G, cast on 12 sts and beg in rib.
Row 1 (WS): (K1, p1) to end.
Row 2: As row 1.
Row 3: P3, (m1, p2) to last st, p1 (16 sts).
Rows 4 to 10: Beg with a k row, work 7 rows in st-st, finishing with a RS row.
Row 11: Cast off 3 sts pwise, p9, cast off rem 3 sts pwise and fasten off (10 sts).
Set aside.
Rep second sleeve as for first sleeve and set aside.

Work right front and right back
Row 47: Rejoin yarn to rem sts and K3, (k2tog) twice, k2, (k2tog) twice, k4 (13 sts).
Row 48: P to last 2 sts, k2.
Row 49: K3, k2tog, k2, k2tog, k4 (11 sts).
Row 50: As row 48.

Work right side of hood
Row 51: K3, (m1, k2) 4 times (15 sts).
Row 52: P to last 2 sts, k2.
Row 53: Knit.
Rows 54 to 75: Rep rows 52 and 53, 11 times more.
Cast off in patt.

SKATEBOARD
(make 2 pieces: one in H and one in I)
Using the long tail method and H or I, cast on 20 sts and work in g-st.
Row 1 (RS): Knit.
Row 2: K1, m1, k to last st, m1, k1 (22 sts).
Rows 3 to 6: Rep rows 1 and 2 twice more (26 sts).
Rows 7 to 10: Work 4 rows in g-st.
Row 11: K2tog, k to last 2 sts, k2tog (24 sts).
Row 12: Knit.
Rows 13 to 15: Rep rows 11 and 12 once then row 11 once (20 sts).
Cast off in g-st.

Wheels (make 2 pieces)
Using the long tail method and C, cast on 8 sts.
Row 1 (WS): Purl.
Row 2: (Kfb) to end (16 sts).
Rows 3 to 13: Beg with a p row, work 11 rows in st-st.
Row 14: (K2tog) to end (8 sts).

Thread yarn through sts on needle, pull tight and secure by threading yarn a second time through sts.

MAKING UP
Note: Sew up all row-end seams on right side using mattress stitch one stitch in from the edge, unless otherwise stated; a one-stitch seam allowance has been allowed for this.

Shoes, legs, body and head
Sew up row ends of shoes. With markers at tips of toes, oversew cast-on stitches; leg seam will be ¼in (6mm) on inside edge of heel. Place a ball of stuffing into toes. Sew up row ends of legs and sew round crotch. Stuff legs, sew up row ends of body and head, and stuff body and head. Pull stitches on a thread tight at top of head and fasten off. To shape neck, take a double piece of yarn to match body and sew a running stitch round last row of body at neck, sewing in and out of every half stitch. Pull tight, knot yarn and sew ends into neck.

Trousers
Sew up leg seams of trousers and sew round crotch. Sew up row ends at centre back and place trousers on doll. Sew cast-off stitches of trousers to first row of upper body all the way round.

Arms and hands
Sew up straight row ends of arms from fingers to underarm and stuff arms using tweezers or tip of scissors.

Leaving armholes open, sew arms to body, sewing top of arms to second row below neck at each side.

Features
Mark position of eyes with two pins on 6th row above neck, spacing two knitted stitches apart. Embroider eyes in black (see page 218 for how to begin and fasten off the embroidery invisibly), making a small chain stitch beginning at marked position and ending on row above, work a second chain stitch on top of first. Embroider mouth in red, making a shallow 'V' shape on the 2nd and 3rd rows below eyes. Shade cheeks with a red pencil.

Hair
Oversew row ends of hair and place on doll and pull hair down to neck at back. Sew in place using back stitch along outside edge.

Hoodie
Sew up sleeve seams of hoodie and sew across under arm. Sew up row ends of hood at back of head and sew up cast-off stitches across top. Place hoodie on doll and sew up back seam.

Skateboard
Using piece of thick cardboard, draw round skateboard and cut out shape inside this line. Sandwich cardboard shape between sides of skateboard and oversew round outside edge of skateboard enclosing cardboard inside. Using ginger, embroider chain stitch around outside edge of skateboard. Sew up row ends of wheels and stuff wheels using tweezers or tip of scissors. Gather round cast-on stitches of wheels, pull tight and secure. Using white, sew a running stitch round centre of wheels to divide into two. Pull tight, wind yarn tightly around centre and knot ends. Sew wheels to underneath of skateboard.

Cowboy

Materials

- ♥ Any DK (US: light worsted) yarn
  (amounts given are approximate):
  5g black (A)
  5g pale pink (B)
  5g grey (C)
  5g white (D)
  5g medium blue (E)
  5g brown (F)
  5g red (G)
  5g pale brown (H)
  2g dark brown (I)
- ♥ Oddments of black, red and yellow for
  embroidery and pale brown for making up
- ♥ 1 pair of 3.25mm (UK10:US3) needles and
  a spare needle of the same size
- ♥ Knitters' pins and a blunt-ended needle
  for sewing up
- ♥ Tweezers (optional)
- ♥ Acrylic toy stuffing
- ♥ A red pencil for shading cheeks

Finished size

Cowboy stands 6½in (16.5cm) tall

Tension

26 sts x 34 rows measure 4in (10cm)
square over st-st using 3.25mm needles
and DK yarn before stuffing

Abbreviations

See page 219

How to make Cowboy

BOOTS, LEGS, BODY AND HEAD
Right leg
Using the long tail method and A for boot, cast on 14 sts.
Place a marker on cast-on edge between the 5th and 6th st of the sts just cast on.
Row 1 (WS): Purl.
Row 2: K2, (m1, k2) to end (20 sts).
Rows 3 to 5: Beg with a p row, work 3 rows in st-st.
Row 6: K2, (k2tog) 6 times, k6 (14 sts).
Row 7: P7, p2tog, p1, p2tog, p2 (12 sts).
Rows 8 and 9: Work 2 rows in st-st.
Rows 10 to 21: Change to B for leg and work 12 rows in st-st.
Break yarn and set aside.

Left leg
Using the long tail method and A for boot, cast on 14 sts.
Place a marker on cast-on edge between the 9th and 10th st of the sts just cast on.
Row 1 (WS): Purl.
Row 2: K2, (m1, k2) to end (20 sts).
Rows 3 to 5: Beg with a p row, work 3 rows in st-st.
Row 6: K6, (k2tog) 6 times, k2 (14 sts).
Row 7: P2, p2tog, p1, p2tog, p7 (12 sts).
Rows 8 and 9: Work 2 rows in st-st.
Rows 10 to 21: Change to B for leg and work 12 rows in st-st.

Join legs
Row 22: Change to C for lower body and with RS facing, k across sts of left leg then with the same yarn cont k across sts of right leg (24 sts).
Rows 23 to 27: Beg with a p row, work 5 rows in st-st.
Rows 28 to 37: Change to D for upper body and work 10 rows in st-st.
Rows 38 and 39: Change to B for head and work 2 rows in st-st.
Row 40: K2, (m1, k4) to last 2 sts, m1, k2 (30 sts).
Rows 41 to 49: Beg with a p row, work 9 rows in st-st.
Row 50: (K2tog, k1) to end (20 sts).
Row 51: Purl.
Row 52: (K2tog) to end (10 sts).
Thread yarn through sts on needle and leave loose.

TROUSERS AND BELT
First leg
Beg at lower edge using the long tail method and E, cast on 21 sts.
Row 1 (RS): Purl.
Rows 2 to 12: Beg with a p row, work 11 rows in st-st.
Rows 13 and 14: Cast off 2 sts at beg of next 2 rows (17 sts).
Break yarn and set aside.

Second leg
Work second leg as for first leg but do not break yarn.

Join legs
Row 15: With RS facing, k across sts of second leg then with the same yarn cont k across sts of first leg (34 sts).
Rows 16 to 18: Beg with a p row, work 3 rows in st-st.
Rows 19 and 20: Change to C for belt and work 2 rows in g-st.
Cast off pwise.

SLEEVES AND HANDS
(make 2)
Beg at shoulder using the long tail method and D, cast on 5 sts.
Row 1 (WS): Purl.
Row 2: K1, (m1, k1) to end (9 sts).
Row 3: Purl.
Row 4: K1, m1, k to last st, m1, k1 (11 sts).
Rows 5 and 6: Rep rows 3 and 4 once (13 sts).
Rows 7 to 13: Beg with a p row, work 7 rows in st-st.
Change to B for hand and dec:
Row 14: K3, (k2tog, k3) twice (11 sts).
Rows 15 to 17: Beg with a p row, work 3 rows in st-st.
Row 18: K2tog, (k1, k2tog) to end (7 sts).
Thread yarn through sts on needle, pull tight and secure by threading yarn a second time through sts.

CUFFS (make 2)
Using the long tail method and D, cast on 14 sts, RS facing to beg.
Cast off pwise.

HAIR
Make hair in F, as for Skateboarder on page 14.

NECKERCHIEF
Using the long tail method and G, cast on 35 sts and work in g-st.
Row 1 (RS): K2tog, k to last 2 sts, k2tog (33 sts).
Row 2: Cast off 14 sts kwise, k12 (13 sts now on RH needle), cast off rem 6 sts and fasten off (13 sts).
Rejoin yarn to rem sts and dec:
Row 3: K2tog, k to last 2 sts, k2tog (11 sts).
Rows 4 to 7: Rep row 3, 4 times more (3 sts).
Row 8: K3tog tbl.
Fasten off.

HAT

Beg at brim using the long tail method and H, cast on 50 sts and beg in g-st, RS facing to beg.

Rows 1 to 5: Work 5 rows in g-st.
Row 6: *(K2tog) 3 times, (k1, k2tog) 5 times, (k2tog) twice; rep from * once (30 sts).
Rows 7 and 8: Join on I for hatband and p 1 row then k 1 row.
Rows 9 to 13: Cont in H and beg with a p row, work 5 rows in st-st.
Row 14: *(K2tog) twice, k7, (k2tog) twice; rep from * once (22 sts).
Row 15: Purl.
Row 16: *(K2tog) twice, k3, (k2tog) twice; rep from * once (14 sts).
Row 17: (P2tog, p3, p2tog) twice (10 sts).
Cast off.

MAKING UP

Note: Sew up all row-end seams on right side using mattress stitch one stitch in from the edge, unless otherwise stated; a one-stitch seam allowance has been allowed for this.

Boots, legs, body and head

Sew up row ends of boots. With markers at tips of toes, oversew cast-on stitches; leg seam will be ¼in (6mm) on inside edge of heel. Place a ball of stuffing into toes. Sew up row ends of legs and sew round crotch. Stuff legs, sew up row ends of body and head, and stuff body and head. Pull stitches on a thread tight at top of head and fasten off. To shape neck, take a double piece of yarn to match body and sew a running stitch round last row of body at neck, sewing in and out of every half stitch. Pull tight, knot yarn and sew ends into neck.

Trousers and belt

Sew up leg seams of trousers and sew round crotch. Sew up row ends at centre back and place trousers on doll. Sew belt of trousers to first row of upper body all the way round.

Sleeves, hands and cuffs

Sew up straight row ends of arms from fingers to underarm and stuff arms using tweezers or tip of scissors. Place cuffs around wrists and oversew row ends. Sew cuffs to wrists all the way round. Leaving armholes open, sew arms to body, sewing top of arms to second row below neck at each side.

Features and hair

Work features and make up hair, as for Skateboarder on page 15.

Neckerchief

Place neckerchief around neck and using red yarn, wind tightly around two ends, ⅓in (8mm) from ends. Sew neckerchief to neck all the way round.

Hat

Fold cast-off stitches in half and oversew. Sew up row ends of hat, stuff top of hat lightly and place hat on head. Pin hat to head and sew in place using back stitch at base of brim, sewing through hat to head all the way round. Turn brim up at sides and stitch in place.

Buckle and lasso

Embroider buckle in yellow at centre front of trousers, making four straight double stitches (see page 218 for how to begin and fasten off the embroidery invisibly). For lasso, make a twisted cord (see page 218) out of one strand of pale brown, beginning with the yarn 60in (150cm) long. Tie a knot 20in (50cm) from folded end and trim ends beyond knot. Thread folded end of lasso through a needle and take a large stitch through knitting, coming up at right hand. Allow knot to disappear through knitting and be caught in the stuffing. Wind lasso three times round three fingers and sew this coil securely to right hand with a double stitch. Sew loose end of lasso to left hand.

Valentine

Materials

- ♥ Any DK (US: light worsted) yarn (amounts given are approximate):
  5g burgundy (A)
  5g pale pink (B)
  5g white (C)
  10g red (D)
  5g cream (E)
  5g brown (F)
- ♥ Oddments of black and red for embroidery and red for making up
- ♥ 1 pair of 3.25mm (UK10:US3) needles and a spare needle of the same size
- ♥ Knitters' pins and a blunt-ended needle for sewing up
- ♥ Tweezers (optional)
- ♥ Acrylic toy stuffing
- ♥ A red pencil for shading cheeks

Finished size

Valentine stands 6$\frac{1}{2}$in (16.5cm) tall

Tension

26 sts x 34 rows measure 4in (10cm) square over st-st using 3.25mm needles and DK yarn before stuffing

Abbreviations

See page 219

How to make Valentine

SLIPPERS, LEGS, BODY AND HEAD

Right leg

Using the long tail method and A for slipper, cast on 14 sts.

Place a marker on cast-on edge between the 5th and 6th st of the sts just cast on.

Row 1 (WS): Purl.

Row 2: K2, (m1, k2) to end (20 sts).

Rows 3 and 4: P 1 row then k 1 row.

Row 5: Change to B and p 1 row.

Row 6: K2, (k2tog) 6 times, k6 (14 sts).

Row 7: P7, p2tog, p1, p2tog, p2 (12 sts).

Rows 8 to 21: Work 14 rows in st-st. Break yarn and set aside.

Left leg

Using the long tail method and A for slipper, cast on 14 sts.

Place a marker on cast-on edge between the 9th and 10th st of the sts just cast on.

Row 1 (WS): Purl.

Row 2: K2, (m1, k2) to end (20 sts).

Rows 3 and 4: P 1 row then k 1 row.

Row 5: Change to B and p 1 row.

Row 6: K6, (k2tog) 6 times, k2 (14 sts).

Row 7: P2, p2tog, p1, p2tog, p7 (12 sts).

Rows 8 to 21: Work 14 rows in st-st.

Join legs

Row 22: Change to C for lower body and with RS facing, k across sts of left leg then with the same yarn cont k across sts of right leg (24 sts).

Rows 23 to 27: Beg with a p row, work 5 rows in st-st.

Rows 28 to 37: Change to D for upper body and work 10 rows in st-st.

Rows 38 and 39: Change to B for head and work 2 rows in st-st.

Row 40: K2, (m1, k4) to last 2 sts, m1, k2 (30 sts).

Rows 41 to 49: Beg with a p row, work 9 rows in st-st.

Row 50: (K2tog, k1) to end (20 sts).

Row 51: Purl.

Row 52: (K2tog) to end (10 sts). Thread yarn through sts on needle and leave loose.

SKIRT

Beg at lower edge using the long tail method and E, cast on 50 sts, WS facing to beg.

Rows 1 and 2: P 1 row then k 1 row (this part is turned under).

Row 3 (picot edge): P1, k1, (yrn, k2tog) to end.

Rows 4 and 5: K 1 row then p 1 row.

Rows 6 to 9: Change to D and work 4 rows in g-st.

Rows 10 to 15: Beg with a k row, work 6 rows in st-st.

Row 16: (K2tog, k3) to end (40 sts).

Rows 17 to 19: Beg with a p row, work 3 rows in st-st.

Row 20: (K2tog, k2) to end (30 sts). Cast off pwise.

SLEEVES, HANDS AND CUFFS

Make sleeves, hands and cuffs beg in D for sleeve and change to B for hand and make cuffs in D, as for Cowboy on page 18.

NECK FRILL
Using the long tail method and D, cast on 40 sts.
Row 1 (WS): (K2, p2) to end.
Cast off in k2, p2 rib.

HAIR
Using the long tail method and F, cast on 6 sts and work in g-st, RS facing to beg.
Row 1 and foll alt row: Knit.
Row 2: (K1, m1) twice, K2, (m1, k1) twice (10 sts).
Row 4: (K1, m1) 4 times, k2, (m1, k1) 4 times (18 sts).
Row 5: Knit.
Row 6: K1, m1, k to last st, m1, k1 (20 sts).
Rows 7 to 18: Rep rows 5 and 6, 6 times more (32 sts).
Rows 19 and 20: Work 2 rows in g-st.
Row 21: (K2tog, k2) 4 times, (k2, k2tog) 4 times (24 sts).
Row 22 and foll alt row: Knit.
Row 23: (K2tog, k1) 4 times, (k1, k2tog) 4 times (16 sts).
Row 25: (K2tog) to end (8 sts).
Row 26: Knit.
Thread yarn through sts on needle, pull tight and secure by threading yarn a second time through sts.

Ringlets (make 4)
Using the long tail method and F, cast on 6 sts and work in rev st-st, RS facing to beg.
Rows 1 to 5: Beg with a p row, work 5 rows in rev st-st.
Thread yarn through sts on needle, pull tight and secure by threading yarn a second time through sts.

Roses (make 2)
Using the long tail method and D, cast on 10 sts.
Thread yarn through sts on needle, pull tight and secure by threading yarn a second time through sts.

HAT
Beg at brim using the long tail method and D, cast on 48 sts and beg in g-st, RS facing to beg.
Rows 1 and 2: Work 2 rows in g-st.
Row 3: (K2tog, k2) to end (36 sts).
Row 4: Knit.
Change to A for hatband and dec:
Row 5: (K2tog, k1) to end (24 sts).
Rows 6 to 8: Work 3 rows in g-st.
Row 9: Cont in D and beg with a k row, work 4 rows in st-st.
Row 10: (K2tog, k1) to end (16 sts).
Row 11: Purl.
Row 12: (K2tog) to end (8 sts).
Thread yarn through sts on needle, pull tight and secure by threading yarn a second time through sts.

Hat bow
Using the long tail method and D, cast on 6 sts and work in g-st, RS facing to beg.
Rows 1 to 3: Work 3 rows in g-st.
Cast off in g-st.

HEART (make 2 pieces)
Using the long tail method and D, cast on 2 sts.
Row 1 (WS): Purl.
Row 2: (Kfb) twice (4 sts).
Row 3: Purl.
Row 4: K1, m1, k to last st, m1, k1 (6 sts).
Rows 5 to 10: Rep rows 3 and 4, 3 times more (12 sts).
Row 11: Purl.
Row 12: K6, turn and work on these 6 sts.
Row 13: Purl.
Row 14: K2tog, k2, k2tog (4 sts).
Row 15: P2tog tbl, p2tog (2 sts).
Thread yarn through sts on needle, pull tight and secure by threading yarn a second time through sts.
Row 16: Rejoin yarn to rem sts and k to end.
Rows 17 to 19: Rep from row 13 to match other side.

Features
Work features, as for Skateboarder on page 15.

Neck frill
Place neck frill around neck and oversew row ends. Sew neck frill to neck all the way round.

Hair
Oversew row ends of hair from crown to end of decrease stitches at forehead. Place hair on doll and pull hair down to neck at back. Sew in place using back stitch along outside edge.

Ringlets and roses
Oversew row ends of ringlets and sew two ringlets together then sew to one side of hair. Repeat for other side. Sew together row ends of roses and sew a rose to top of ringlets at each side.

Hat and hat bow
Sew up row ends of hat and stuff top lightly. Pin hat to head and sew in place using back stitch at base of brim, sewing through hat to head all the way round. To make bow, wind yarn to match bow around centre of bow tightly and tie at back. Sew bow to hatband at side.

Heart
Place wrong sides of heart pieces together, matching all edges, then sew around outside edge leaving a gap. Stuff heart and sew up gap. Place frill around outside edge of heart, oversew row ends and stitch frill around heart. Sew heart to hands.

Dress bow
Shape bow into bow shape, stitch together and sew to waist at back of skirt.

Frill
Using the long tail method and E, cast on 44 sts and work in 2 x 2 rib.
Row 1 (WS): (K2, p2) to end.
Cast off in 2 x 2 rib.

DRESS BOW
Using the long tail method and D, cast on 30 sts.
Cast off kwise.

MAKING UP
Note: Sew up all row-end seams on right side using mattress stitch one stitch in from the edge, unless otherwise stated; a one-stitch seam allowance has been allowed for this.

Slippers, legs, body and head
Sew up row ends of slippers and ankles. With markers at tips of toes, oversew cast-on stitches; leg seam will be ¼in (6mm) on inside edge of heel. Place a ball of stuffing into toes. Sew up row ends of legs and sew round crotch. Stuff legs, sew up row ends of body and head, and stuff body and head. Pull stitches on a thread tight at top of head and fasten off. To shape neck, take a double length of yarn to match body and sew a running stitch round last row of body at neck, sewing in and out of every half stitch. Pull tight, knot yarn and sew ends into neck.

Skirt
Sew up row ends of skirt. Fold picot edge under and hem in place. Place skirt on doll and sew cast-off stitches of skirt to first row of upper body all the way round.

Sleeves, hands and cuffs
Sew up straight row ends of arms from fingers to underarm and stuff arms using tweezers or tip of scissors. Place cuffs around wrists and oversew row ends. Sew cuffs to wrists all the way round. Leaving armholes open, sew arms to body with arms sloping forwards.

Firefighter

Materials

- Any DK (US: light worsted) yarn (amounts given are approximate):
  10g black (A)
  5g pale pink (B)
  5g white (C)
  5g silver grey (D)
  5g brown (E)
  5g yellow (F)
  5g dark grey (G)
  10g burnt orange (H)
- Oddments of black, red and white for embroidery
- 1 pair of 3.25mm (UK10:US3) needles and a spare needle of the same size
- Knitters' pins and a blunt-ended needle for sewing up
- Tweezers (optional)
- Acrylic toy stuffing
- A red pencil for shading cheeks

Finished size

Firefighter stands 6½in (16.5cm) tall

Tension

26 sts x 34 rows measure 4in (10cm) square over st-st using 3.25mm needles and DK yarn before stuffing

Abbreviations

See page 219

How to make Firefighter

BOOTS, LEGS, BODY AND HEAD

Make boots, legs, body and head using A for boots, B for legs, C for lower body, A for upper body and B for head, as for Cowboy on page 17.

TROUSERS

First leg

Beg at lower edge using the long tail method and A, cast on 21 sts, RS facing to beg.

Rows 1 and 2: P 2 rows.

Rows 3 to 5: Join on D and k 2 rows then p 1 row.

Rows 6 to 14: Change to A and beg with a p row, work 9 rows in st-st.

Rows 15 and 16: Cast off 2 sts at beg of next 2 rows (17 sts).

Break yarn and set aside.

Second leg

Work second leg as for first leg but do not break yarn.

Join legs

Row 17: With RS facing, k across sts of second leg then with the same yarn cont k across sts of first leg (34 sts).

Rows 18 to 22: Beg with a p row, work 5 rows in st-st.

Cast off.

Trim on trousers (make 2 pieces)

Using the long tail method and D, cast on 14 sts, RS facing to beg.

Cast off pwise.

ARMS AND HAIR

Make arms in B and hair in E, as for Skateboarder on pages 13 and 14.

JACKET

Note: Sleeves are worked first and knitted into body.

Sleeves (make 2)

Beg at cuff using the long tail method and A, cast on 16 sts, RS facing to beg.

Rows 1 and 2: P 2 rows.

Rows 3 to 5: Join on D and k 2 rows then p 1 row.

Rows 6 to 11: Change to A and beg with a p row, work 6 rows in st-st, finishing with a RS row.

Row 12: Cast off 3 sts pwise, p9, cast off rem 3 sts pwise and fasten off (10 sts).

Set aside.

Rep second sleeve as for first sleeve and set aside.

Front and back

Using the long tail method and A, cast on 38 sts, RS facing to beg.

Rows 1 and 2: P 2 rows.

Rows 3 to 5: Join on D and k 2 rows then p 1 row.

Row 6: Change to A and p 1 row.

Rows 7 to 11: Beg with a k row, work 5 rows in st-st and k the first 2 sts and the last 2 sts on every p row, finishing with a RS row.

Divide for armholes

Row 12: K2, p6, cast off 4 sts pwise, p13, cast off 4 sts pwise, p5, k2 (30 sts).

Join sleeves

Row 13: Change to D and with RS of all pieces facing, k8 from right front, k10 from one sleeve, k14 across back, k10 from other sleeve, k8 from left front (50 sts).
Row 14: K6, (k2tog) twice, k6, (k2tog) twice, k10, (k2tog) twice, k6, (k2tog) twice, k6 (42 sts).
Row 15: P5, (p2tog) twice, p4, (p2tog) twice, p8, (p2tog) twice, p4, (p2tog) twice, p5 (34 sts).
Row 16: Change to A and p 1 row.
Row 17: K4, (k2tog) twice, k2, (k2tog) twice, k6, (k2tog) twice, k2, (k2tog) twice, k4 (26 sts).

Row 18: K2, p to last st, k2.
Row 19: P 1 row.
Cast off kwise.

Trim on jacket (make 4 pieces)

Using the long tail method and D, cast on 6 sts, RS facing to beg.
Cast off pwise.

HAT

Using the long tail method and F, cast on 48 sts and beg in g-st, RS facing to beg.
Rows 1 to 4: Work 4 rows in g-st.
Row 5: (K2tog, k2) to end (36 sts).
Rows 6 to 14: Beg with a p row, work 9 rows in st-st.
Row 15: (K2tog, k1) to end (24 sts).
Row 16 and foll alt row: Purl.
Row 17: (K2tog, k1) to end (16 sts).

Row 19: (K2tog) to end (8 sts).
Thread yarn through sts on needle, pull tight and secure by threading yarn a second time through sts.

HOSE

Using the long tail method and G, cast on 10 sts, RS facing to beg.
Rows 1 and 2: K 1 row then p 1 row.
Row 3: K1, m1, k to end (11 sts).
Row 4: P 1 row.
Rows 5 to 10: Rep rows 3 and 4, 3 times more (14 sts).
Rows 11 to 14: Work 4 rows in g-st.
Change to H and beg with a k row, work in st-st for 8in (20cm) or required length.
Cast off.

MAKING UP

Note: Sew up all row-end seams on right side using mattress stitch one stitch in from the edge, unless otherwise stated; a one-stitch seam allowance has been allowed for this.

Boots, legs, body and head

Make up boots, legs, body and head, as for Cowboy on page 19.

Trousers

Sew up leg seams of trousers and sew round crotch. Sew up row ends at centre back and place trousers on doll. Sew cast-off stitches of trousers to first row of upper body all the way round. Place trim on sides of trousers and sew edges down.

Arms, features and hair

Make up arms, work features and make up hair, as for Skateboarder on page 15.

Jacket

Sew up sleeve seams of jacket and sew across under arm. Place jacket on doll and sew together down centre front. Place trim on front and back of jacket and sew all edges down.

Hat

Sew up row ends of hat and stuff top of hat. Pin hat to head and sew in place using back stitch at base of brim, sewing through hat to head all the way round. Using picture as a guide, embroider badge in white and red at front of hat.

Hose

Roll hose up from row ends to row ends and stitch down along length. Sew hose to hand of Firefighter.

Painter & Decorator

Materials

- Any DK (US: light worsted) yarn
  (amounts given are approximate):
  5g black (A)
  10g white (B)
  5g grey (C)
  5g pale pink (D)
  5g brown (E)
  5g navy blue (F)
  5g burnt orange (G)
  2g dark brown (H)
  2g fawn (I)
- Oddments of black, red, blue and yellow
  for embroidery
- 1 pair of 3.25mm (UK10:US3) needles and
  a spare needle of the same size
- Knitters' pins and a blunt-ended needle for
  sewing up
- Tweezers (optional)
- Acrylic toy stuffing
- A red pencil for shading cheeks

Finished size

Painter & Decorator stands 6in (15cm) tall

Tension

26 sts x 34 rows measure 4in (10cm)
square over st-st using 3.25mm needles
and DK yarn before stuffing

Abbreviations

See page 219

How to make Painter & Decorator

BOOTS, LEGS, BODY AND HEAD
Right leg
Using the long tail method and A for boot, cast on 14 sts.
Place a marker on cast-on edge between the 5th and 6th st of the sts just cast on.
Row 1 (WS): Purl.
Row 2: K2, (m1, k2) to end (20 sts).
Rows 3 to 5: Beg with a p row, work 3 rows in st-st.
Row 6: K2, (k2tog) 6 times, k6 (14 sts).
Row 7: P7, p2tog, p1, p2tog, p2 (12 sts).
Rows 8 and 9: Work 2 rows in st-st.
Rows 10 to 21: Change to B for leg and work 12 rows in st-st.
Break yarn and set aside.

Left leg
Using the long tail method and A for boot, cast on 14 sts.

Place a marker on cast-on edge between the 9th and 10th st of the sts just cast on.
Row 1 (WS): Purl.
Row 2: K2, (m1, k2) to end (20 sts).
Rows 3 to 5: Beg with a p row, work 3 rows in st-st.
Row 6: K6, (k2tog) 6 times, k2 (14 sts).
Row 7: P2, p2tog, p1, p2tog, p7 (12 sts).
Rows 8 and 9: Work 2 rows in st-st.
Rows 10 to 21: Change to B for leg and work 12 rows in st-st.

Join legs
Row 22: With RS facing, k across sts of left leg then with the same yarn cont k across sts of right leg (24 sts).
Place a marker on first and last st of last row.
Rows 23 to 27: Beg with a p row, work 5 rows in st-st.

Rows 28 to 37: Change to C for upper body and work 10 rows in st-st.
Rows 38 and 39: Change to D for head and work 2 rows in st-st.
Row 40: K2, (m1, k4) to last 2 sts, m1, k2 (30 sts).
Rows 41 to 49: Beg with a p row, work 9 rows in st-st.
Row 50: (K2tog, k1) to end (20 sts).
Row 51: Purl.
Row 52: (K2tog) to end (10 sts).
Thread yarn through sts on needle and leave loose.

SLEEVES, ARMS AND HANDS (make 2)
Beg at shoulder using the long tail method and C, cast on 4 sts.
Row 1 (WS): Purl.
Row 2: K1, (m1, k1) to end (7 sts).
Row 3: Purl.
Row 4: K1, m1, k to last st, m1, k1 (9 sts).
Rows 5 and 6: Rep rows 3 and 4 once (11 sts).
Rows 7 to 13: Change to D for arm and beg with a p row, work 7 rows in st-st.
Place a marker on last row for wrist gathering.
Rows 14 to 17: Work 4 rows in st-st.
Row 18: K2tog, (k1, k2tog) to end (7 sts).
Thread yarn through sts on needle, pull tight and secure by threading yarn a second time through sts.

ARM CUFFS (make 2)
Using the long tail method and C, cast on 16 sts, RS facing to beg.
Cast off pwise.

HAIR
Make hair in E, as for Skateboarder on page 14.

DUNGAREES

First leg
Beg at lower edge using the long tail method and B, cast on 21 sts.
Row 1 (RS): Purl.
Rows 2 to 12: Beg with a p row, work 11 rows in st-st.
Rows 13 and 14: Cast off 2 sts at beg of next 2 rows (17 sts).
Break yarn and set aside.

Second leg
Work second leg as for first leg but do not break yarn.

Join legs
Row 15: With RS facing, k across sts of second leg then with the same yarn cont k across sts of first leg (34 sts).
Rows 16 to 20: Beg with a p row, work 5 rows in st-st.
Row 21: Purl.

Divide for bib
Row 22: Cast off 13 sts kwise, k7, cast off rem sts kwise (8 sts).
Break yarn and rejoin to rem sts.
Row 23: Knit.
Row 24: K2, p4, k2.
Rows 25 to 28: Rep rows 23 and 24 twice more.
Row 29: Purl.
Cast off kwise.

Straps (make 2)
Using the long tail method and B, cast on 20 sts, RS facing to beg.
Cast off pwise.

CAP
Using the long tail method and F, cast on 36 sts.
Row 1 (RS): Knit.
Row 2: P2, (m1, p4) to last 2 sts, m1, p2 (45 sts).
Rows 3 to 8: Beg with a k row, work 6 rows in st-st.
Row 9: (K2tog, k3) to end (36 sts).
Row 10 and foll 2 alt rows: Purl.
Row 11: (K2tog, k2) to end (27 sts).

Row 13: (K2tog, k1) to end (18 sts).
Row 15: (K2tog) to end (9 sts).
Thread yarn through sts on needle, pull tight and secure by threading yarn a second time through sts.

Peak
Using the long tail method and F, cast on 10 sts, WS facing to beg.
Rows 1 and 2: P 1 row then k 1 row.
Row 3: P8, turn.
Row 4: S1k, k5, turn.
Row 5: S1p, p to end.
Row 6: Knit.
Rows 7 to 10: Rep rows 3 to 6 once.
Row 11: Purl.
Cast off.

PAINT POT
Beg at base, using the long tail method and G, cast on 9 sts, WS facing to beg.
Row 1 and foll alt row: Purl.
Row 2: K1, (m1, k1) to end (17 sts).

Row 4: K1, (m1, k2) to end (25 sts).
Rows 5 and 6: K 1 row then p 1 row.
Rows 7 to 11: Beg with a p row, work 5 rows in st-st.
Rows 12 and 13: P 1 row then k 1 row.
Change to B and dec:
Row 14: K1, (k2tog, k1) to end (17 sts).
Row 15: Purl.
Row 16: K1, (k2tog) to end (9 sts).
Thread yarn through sts on needle, pull tight and secure by threading yarn a second time through sts.

Handle (make 2 pieces)
Using the long tail method and G, cast on 15 sts, RS facing to beg.
Cast off pwise.

BRUSH
Using the long tail method and H, cast on 12 sts.
Row 1 (WS): Purl.
Row 2: (K1, m1, k4, m1, k1) twice (16 sts).

wrist. Pull tight, knot yarn and sew ends into wrists. Leaving armholes open, sew arms to body, sewing top of arms to second row below neck at each side.

Features and hair
Work features and make up hair, as for Skateboarder on page 15.

Dungarees, straps and embroidery
Sew up leg seams of dungarees and sew round crotch. Sew up row ends at centre back and place dungarees on doll. Sew waist of dungarees to first row of upper body all the way round. Sew ends of straps to bib, take straps over shoulders and cross over and sew to waist of dungarees at back. Embroider paint splashes on dungarees in blue, yellow and red, making short stitches.

Cap
Sew up row ends of cap and place on head. Sew lower edge of cap to head all the way round. Fold peak, bringing cast-on and cast-off stitches together, and oversew this edge. Gather row ends, pull tight and secure. Sew peak to front of cap.

Paint pot and brush
Gather round cast-on stitches of paint pot, pull tight and secure. Sew up row ends of paint pot leaving a gap, stuff and sew up gap. Place two pieces of handle together, matching all edges, and oversew around outside edge. Sew handle to paint pot and to left hand of doll. Fold cast-on stitches of brush in half and oversew. Fold cast-off stitches of brush in half and oversew. Stuff brush very lightly, keeping flat. Sew cast-on and cast-off stitches of brush handle together along length and sew end to brush. Sew brush to right hand of doll.

Rows 3 to 5: P 2 rows then k 1 row.
Rows 6 to 8: Change to I and beg with a k row, work 3 rows in st-st, finishing with a RS row.
Row 9: Change to B and p 1 row.
Row 10: K1, (p1, k1) to end.
Cast off in k1, p1 moss-st.

Handle
Using the long tail method and H, cast on 5 sts, WS facing to beg.
Rows 1 to 3: Beg with a p row, work 3 rows in st-st.
Cast off.

MAKING UP
Note: Sew up all row-end seams on right side using mattress stitch one stitch in from the edge, unless otherwise stated; a one-stitch seam allowance has been allowed for this.

Boots, legs, body and head
Sew up row ends of boots and with markers at tips of toes, oversew cast-on stitches; leg seam will be ¼in

(6mm) on inside edge of heel. Place a ball of stuffing into toes and sew up row ends of legs. Bring markers together at crotch and sew round crotch. Stuff legs, sew up row ends of body and head, and stuff body and head. Pull stitches on a thread tight at top of head and fasten off. To shape neck, take a double piece of yarn to match body and sew a running stitch round last row of body at neck, sewing in and out of every half stitch. Pull tight, knot yarn and sew ends into neck.

Sleeves, arms, hands and arm cuffs
Sew up straight row ends of arms and sleeves from fingers to underarm and stuff arms using tweezers or tip of scissors. Place arm cuffs around arms and oversew row ends. Sew arm cuffs to arms all the way round. To shape wrists, take a double length of pale pink yarn and sew a running stitch round row with marker at

Ballerina

Materials

- ♥ Any DK (US: light worsted) yarn (amounts given are approximate):
  5g bright pink (A)
  5g pale pink (B)
  5g medium pink (C)
  5g fawn (D)
- ♥ Oddments of black, red, and bright pink for embroidery
- ♥ 1 pair of 3.25mm (UK10:US3) needles and a spare needle of the same size
- ♥ Knitters' pins and a blunt-ended needle for sewing up
- ♥ Tweezers (optional)
- ♥ Acrylic toy stuffing
- ♥ A red pencil for shading cheeks

Finished size

Ballerina stands 6½in (16.5cm) tall

Tension

26 sts x 34 rows measure 4in (10cm) square over st-st using 3.25mm needles and DK yarn before stuffing

Abbreviations

See page 219

How to make Ballerina

SHOES, LEGS, BODY AND HEAD
Right leg
Using the long tail method and A for shoe, cast on 14 sts.
Place a marker on cast-on edge between the 5th and 6th st of the sts just cast on.
Row 1 (WS): Purl.
Row 2: K2, (m1, k2) to end (20 sts).
Row 3: Purl.
Rows 4 and 5: Change to B for leg and k 1 row then p 1 row.
Row 6: K2, (k2tog) 6 times, k6 (14 sts).
Row 7: P7, p2tog, p1, p2tog, p2 (12 sts).
Rows 8 to 21: Work 14 rows in st-st. Break yarn and set aside.

Left leg
Using the long tail method and A for shoe, cast on 14 sts.
Place a marker on cast-on edge between the 9th and 10th st of the sts just cast on.
Row 1 (WS): Purl.
Row 2: K2, (m1, k2) to end (20 sts).
Row 3: Purl.
Rows 4 and 5: Change to B for leg and k 1 row then p 1 row.
Row 6: K6, (k2tog) 6 times, k2 (14 sts).
Row 7: P2, p2tog, p1, p2tog, p7 (12 sts).
Rows 8 to 21: Work 14 rows in st-st.

Join legs
Row 22: With RS facing, k across sts of left leg then with the same yarn cont k across sts of right leg (24 sts). Place a marker on first and last st of last row.
Rows 23 to 25: Beg with a p row, work 3 rows in st-st.
Rows 26 to 33: Change to A for upper body and work 8 rows in st-st.
Rows 34 to 37: Change to B for neck and work 4 rows in st-st. Place a marker on last row for neck gathering.

Rows 38 and 39: Work 2 rows in st-st.
Row 40: K2, (m1, k4) to last 2 sts, m1, k2 (30 sts).
Rows 41 to 49: Beg with a p row, work 9 rows in st-st.
Row 50: (K2tog, k1) to end (20 sts).
Row 51: Purl.
Row 52: (K2tog) to end (10 sts).
Thread yarn through sts on needle and leave loose.

LOWER LEOTARD
Beg at front waist edge using the long tail method and A, cast on 15 sts.
Row 1 (WS): Purl.
Row 2: K2tog, k to last 2 sts, k2tog (13 sts).
Row 3: P2tog, p to last 2 sts, p2tog (11 sts).
Rows 4 to 7: Rep rows 2 and 3 twice more (3 sts).
Rows 8 to 11: Work 4 rows in st-st.
Row 12: K1, m1, k1, m1, k1 (5 sts).
Row 13 and foll 2 alt rows: Purl.
Row 14: K1, (m1, k1) to end (9 sts).
Row 16: (K1, m1) twice, k5, (m1, k1) twice (13 sts).
Row 18: K1, m1, k11, m1, k1 (15 sts).
Cast off pwise.

TUTU (make 2 pieces)

Using the long tail method and C, cast on 60 sts and work in g-st, RS facing to beg.

Rows 1 and 2: Work 2 rows in g-st.
Rows 3 to 6: Change to A and work 4 rows in g-st.
Row 7: (K2tog) to end (30 sts).
Cast off in g-st.

ARMS AND HANDS (make 2)

Beg at shoulder using the long tail method and B, cast on 4 sts.
Row 1 (WS): Purl.
Row 2: K1, (m1, k1) to end (7 sts).
Row 3: Purl.
Row 4: K1, m1, k to last st, m1, k1 (9 sts).

Rows 5 and 6: Rep rows 3 and 4 once (11 sts).
Rows 7 to 13: Beg with a p row, work 7 rows in st-st.
Place a marker on last row for wrist gathering.
Rows 14 to 17: Work 4 rows in st-st.
Row 18: K2tog, (k1, k2tog) to end (7 sts).
Thread yarn through sts on needle, pull tight and secure by threading yarn a second time through sts.

NECK EDGING

Using the long tail method and C, cast on 30 sts, RS facing to beg.
Cast off pwise.

HAIR

Make hair in D, as for Valentine on page 22.

Bun

Using the long tail method and D, cast on 12 sts and work in g-st, RS facing to beg.
Rows 1 to 6: Work 6 rows in g-st.
Row 7: (K2tog) to end (6 sts).
Row 8: Knit.
Thread yarn through sts on needle, pull tight and secure by threading yarn a second time through sts.

BOW

Using the long tail method and A, cast on 6 sts and work in g-st, RS facing to beg.
Rows 1 to 3: Work 3 rows in g-st.
Cast off in g-st.

MAKING UP

Note: Sew up all row-end seams on right side using mattress stitch one stitch in from the edge, unless otherwise stated; a one-stitch seam allowance has been allowed for this.

Shoes, legs, body and head

Sew up row ends of shoes and ankles. With markers at tips of toes, oversew cast-on stitches; leg seam will be $\frac{1}{4}$in (6mm) on inside edge of heel. Place a ball of stuffing into toes and sew up row ends of legs. Bring markers together at crotch and sew round crotch. Stuff legs, sew up row ends of body and head, and stuff body and head. Pull stitches on a thread tight at top of head and fasten off. To shape neck, take a double piece of pale pink yarn and sew a running stitch round row with marker at neck, sewing in and out of every half stitch. Pull tight, knot yarn and sew ends into neck.

Lower leotard

Place lower leotard on doll and stitch together straight row ends at each side. Sew waist edge to first row of upper body all the way round.

Tutu

Oversew row ends of both pieces of tutu. With seams at centre back, place on doll and sew first tutu to row above lower leotard and second tutu to row above this.

Arms and hands

Sew up straight row ends of arms from fingers to underarm and stuff arms using tweezers or tip of scissors. To shape wrists, take double length of pale pink yarn and sew a running stitch round row with marker at wrist, sewing in and out of every half stitch. Pull tight, knot yarn and sew ends into wrist. Leaving armholes open, sew arms to body, sewing top of arms to second row below neck at each side.

Neck edging

Place neck edging around neck and oversew row ends. Pin neck edging around top of leotard and over shoulders and sew in place using back stitch down centre of neck edging.

Features and shoe straps

Work features, as for Skateboarder on page 15. Using picture as a guide, embroider shoe straps in bright pink.

Hair and bun

Make up hair, as for Valentine on page 23. To make bun, oversew row ends of bun and stuff bun. Sew cast-on stitches of bun to top of head.

Bow

To shape bow, wind matching yarn tightly around middle of bow and knot at back. Sew bow to top of head.

Surfer

Materials

- ♥ Any DK (US: light worsted) yarn (amounts given are approximate):
  10g pale pink (A)
  5g white (B)
  5g aqua blue (C)
  5g orange (D)
  10g yellow (E)
  5g brown (F)
  5g grey (G)
- ♥ Oddments of black and red for embroidery and grey for making up
- ♥ 1 pair of 3.25mm (UK10:US3) needles and a spare needle of the same size
- ♥ Knitters' pins and a blunt-ended needle for sewing up
- ♥ Tweezers (optional)
- ♥ Acrylic toy stuffing
- ♥ A red pencil for shading cheeks
- ♥ Piece of thick cardboard 8 x 4in (20 x 10cm)

Finished size

Surfer stands 6in (15cm) tall

Tension

26 sts x 34 rows measure 4in (10cm) square over st-st using 3.25mm needles and DK yarn before stuffing

Abbreviations

See page 219

How to make Surfer

FEET, LEGS, BODY AND HEAD
Right leg
Using the long tail method and A for foot, cast on 14 sts.
Place a marker on cast-on edge between the 5th and 6th st of the sts just cast on.
Row 1 (WS): Purl.
Row 2: K2, (m1, k2) to end (20 sts).
Rows 3 to 5: Beg with a p row, work 3 rows in st-st.
Row 6: K2, (k2tog) 6 times, k6 (14 sts).
Row 7: P7, p2tog, p1, p2tog, p2 (12 sts).
Rows 8 to 21: Work 14 rows in st-st. Break yarn and set aside.

Left leg
Using the long tail method and A for foot, cast on 14 sts.
Place a marker on cast-on edge between the 9th and 10th st of the sts just cast on.
Row 1 (WS): Purl.
Row 2: K2, (m1, k2) to end (20 sts).
Rows 3 to 5: Beg with a p row, work 3 rows in st-st.
Row 6: K6, (k2tog) 6 times, k2 (14 sts).
Row 7: P2, p2tog, p1, p2tog, p7 (12 sts).
Rows 8 to 21: Work 14 rows in st-st.

Join legs
Row 22: Change to B for lower body and with RS facing, k across sts of left leg then with the same yarn cont k across sts of right leg (24 sts).
Rows 23 to 25: Beg with a p row, work 3 rows in st-st.

Rows 26 to 37: Change to A for upper body and work 12 rows in st-st. Place a marker on last row for neck gathering.
Rows 38 and 39: Work 2 rows in st-st.
Row 40: K2, (m1, k4) to last 2 sts, m1, k2 (30 sts).
Rows 41 to 49: Beg with a p row, work 9 rows in st-st.
Row 50: (K2tog, k1) to end (20 sts).
Row 51: Purl.
Row 52: (K2tog) to end (10 sts).
Thread yarn through sts on needle and leave loose.

SHORTS
First leg
Beg at lower edge using the long tail method and C, cast on 21 sts, RS facing to beg.

Rows 1 to 6: Beg with a k row, work 6 rows in st-st.
Rows 7 and 8: Cast off 2 sts at beg of next 2 rows (17 sts). Break yarn and set aside.

Second leg
Work second leg as for first leg but do not break yarn.

Join legs
Row 9: With RS facing, k across sts of second leg then with the same yarn cont k across sts of first leg (34 sts).
Row 10: Change to D and p 1 row.
Rows 11 and 12: Change to E and k 1 row then p 1 row.
Row 13: K2, (m1, k6) to last 2 sts, m1, k2 (40 sts).
Row 14: (K1, p1) to end.
Row 15: As row 14. Cast off in k1, p1 rib.

ARMS AND HANDS
Make arms and hands in A, as for Ballerina on page 34.

HAIR
Make hair in F, as for Skateboarder on page 14.

SURFBOARD (make 2 pieces)
Using the long tail method and E, cast on 12 sts, WS facing to beg.
Rows 1 to 9: Beg with a p row, work 9 rows in st-st.
Row 10: K1, m1, k to last st, m1, k1 (14 sts).
Rows 11 to 30: Rep rows 1 to 10 twice more (18 sts).

Row 31: Purl.
Rows 32 to 37: Change to B and work 6 rows in st-st.
Rows 38 to 41: Change to D and work 4 rows in st-st.
Row 42: K2tog, k to last 2 sts, k2tog (16 sts).
Row 43: Purl.
Rows 44 and 45: Rep rows 42 and 43 once (14 sts).
Row 46: (K2tog) twice, k6, (k2tog) twice (10 sts).
Row 47: P2tog, p6, p2tog (8 sts).
Row 48: (K2tog) to end (4 sts). Cast off pwise.

CUFF
Using the long tail method and G, cast on 11 sts and work in rib, WS facing to beg.
Row 1: K1, (p1, k1) to end.
Row 2: P1, (k1, p1) to end. Cast off in rib.

MAKING UP

Note: Sew up all row-end seams on right side using mattress stitch one stitch in from the edge, unless otherwise stated; a one-stitch seam allowance has been allowed for this.

Feet, legs, body and head

Sew up row ends of feet and ankles. With markers at tips of toes, oversew cast-on stitches; leg seam will be ¼in (6mm) on inside edge of heel. Place a ball of stuffing into toes, sew up row ends of legs and sew round crotch. Stuff legs, sew up row ends of body and head, and stuff body and head. Pull stitches on a thread tight at top of head and fasten off. To shape neck, take a double piece of pale pink yarn and sew a running stitch round row with marker at neck, sewing in and out of every half stitch. Pull tight, knot yarn and sew ends into neck.

Shorts

Sew up row ends of legs of shorts and sew round crotch. Sew up row ends at centre back and place shorts on doll. Sew shorts to first row of upper body using back stitch, sewing through shorts at base of waistband.

Arms and hands

Make up arms and hands, as for Ballerina on page 35.

Features and hair

Work features and make up hair, as for Skateboarder on page 15.

Surfboard and cuff

Make a twisted cord (see page 218) out of one piece of grey yarn, beginning with the yarn 25in (65cm) long. Tie a knot 5in (12.5cm) from folded end and trim ends. Sew knotted end of cord to rear of one piece of surfboard, sewing

through knot on wrong side to secure. Using a piece of thick cardboard, draw around surfboard and cut out shape inside this line. Sandwich cardboard shape between sides of surfboard and sew around outside edge of surfboard, enclosing cardboard inside. Oversew row ends of cuff and sew folded end of cord to cuff securely. Place cuff on wrist of Surfer.

Fairy

Materials

- ♥ Any DK (US: light worsted) yarn
  (amounts given are approximate):
  10g cerise (A)
  5g pale pink (B)
  5g white (C)
  5g yellow (D)
  10g medium pink (E)
- ♥ Oddments of black and red for embroidery
- ♥ 1 pair of 3.25mm (UK10:US3) needles and
  a spare needle of the same size
- ♥ Knitters' pins and a blunt-ended needle
  for sewing up
- ♥ Tweezers (optional)
- ♥ Acrylic toy stuffing
- ♥ 1 chenille stem
- ♥ A red pencil for shading cheeks

Finished size

Fairy stands 6in (15cm) tall

Tension

26 sts x 34 rows measure 4in (10cm)
square over st-st using 3.25mm needles
and DK yarn before stuffing

Abbreviations

See page 219

How to make Fairy

SLIPPERS, LEGS, BODY AND HEAD
Right leg
Using the long tail method and A for slipper, cast on 14 sts.
Place a marker on cast-on edge between the 5th and 6th st of the sts just cast on.
Row 1 (WS): Purl.
Row 2: K2, (m1, k2) to end (20 sts).
Rows 3 and 4: P 1 row then k 1 row.
Row 5: Change to B for leg and p 1 row.
Row 6: K2, (k2tog) 6 times, k6 (14 sts).
Row 7: P7, p2tog, p1, p2tog, p2 (12 sts).
Rows 8 to 21: Work 14 rows in st-st. Break yarn and set aside.

Left leg
Using the long tail method and A for slipper, cast on 14 sts.
Place a marker on cast-on edge between the 9th and 10th st of the sts just cast on.
Row 1 (WS): Purl.
Row 2: K2, (m1, k2) to end (20 sts).
Rows 3 and 4: P 1 row then k 1 row.
Row 5: Change to B for leg and p 1 row.
Row 6: K6, (k2tog) 6 times, k2 (14 sts).
Row 7: P2, p2tog, p1, p2tog, p7 (12 sts).
Rows 8 to 21: Work 14 rows in st-st.

Join legs
Row 22: Change to C for lower body and with RS facing, k across sts of left leg then with the same yarn cont k across sts of right leg (24 sts).
Rows 23 to 27: Beg with a p row, work 5 rows in st-st.
Rows 28 to 33: Change to A for upper body and work 6 rows in st-st.
Rows 34 to 37: Change to B for neck and work 4 rows in st-st.
Place a marker on last row for neck gathering.

Rows 38 and 39: Work 2 rows in st-st.
Row 40: K2, (m1, k4) to last 2 sts, m1, k2 (30 sts).
Rows 41 to 49: Beg with a p row, work 9 rows in st-st.
Row 50: (K2tog, k1) to end (20 sts).
Row 51: Purl.
Row 52: (K2tog) to end (10 sts).
Thread yarn through sts on needle and leave loose.

SKIRT
Beg at lower edge using the long tail method and C, cast on 40 sts, WS facing to beg.
Rows 1 and 2: P 1 row then k 1 row (this part is turned under).
Row 3 (picot edge): P1, k1, (yrn, k2tog) to end.
Rows 4 and 5: K 1 row then p 1 row.
Rows 6 and 7: Change to A and work 2 rows in g-st.
Rows 8 to 13: Beg with a k row, work 6 rows in st-st.
Row 14: (K2tog, k2) to end (30 sts).
Row 15: Purl.
Cast off.

SLEEVES, ARMS AND HANDS
Make sleeves, arms and hands using A for sleeves and B for arms and hands, as for Painter & Decorator on page 29.

Sleeve frills (make 2)
Using the long tail method and C, cast on 16 sts, WS facing to beg.
Rows 1 and 2: P 1 row then k 1 row.
Row 3 (picot edge): P1, k1, (yrn, k2tog) to end.
Rows 4 and 5: K 1 row then p 1 row.
Cast off.

NECK EDGING
Using the long tail method and A, cast on 30 sts, RS facing to beg.
Cast off pwise.

HAIR
Make hair in D, as for Valentine on page 22.

Hair loops (make 4)

Using the long tail method and D, cast on 12 sts, RS facing to beg. Cast off pwise.

WINGS (make 2)

Using the long tail method and E, cast on 16 sts and work in g-st.

Row 1 (RS): Knit.

Row 2: K6, (m1, k1) twice, (k1, m1) twice, k6 (20 sts).

Row 3: Knit.

Row 4: K8, (m1, k1) twice, (k1, m1) twice, k8 (24 sts).

Row 5: Knit.

Row 6: K10, (m1, k1) twice, (k1, m1) twice, k10 (28 sts).

Row 7: Knit.

Row 8: K12, (m1, k1) twice, (k1, m1) twice, k12 (32 sts).

Rows 9 to 12: Work 4 rows in g-st.

Row 13: K10, (k2tog, k1) twice, (k1, k2tog) twice, k10 (28 sts).

Row 14: Knit.

Row 15: K8, (k2tog, k1) twice, (k1, k2tog) twice, k8 (24 sts).

Row 16: Knit.

Row 17: K6, (k2tog, k1) twice, (k1, k2tog) twice, k6 (20 sts).

Rows 18 to 22: Rep rows 4 to 8 once (32 sts).

Row 23: K2tog, k to last 2 sts, k2tog (30 sts).

Rows 24 to 34: Rep row 23, 11 times more (8 sts).

Row 35: (K2tog) to end (4 sts).

Row 36: Knit.

Thread yarn through sts on needle, pull tight and secure by threading yarn a second time through sts.

WAND
Stick

Using the long tail method and E, cast on 6 sts, WS facing to beg. Beg with a p row, work in st-st for 2¼in (5.5cm).

Thread yarn through sts on needle, pull tight and secure by threading yarn a second time through sts.

Head of wand

Using the long tail method and E, cast on 10 sts, WS facing to beg.

Rows 1 and 2: P 1 row then k 1 row.

Row 3 (picot row): P1, k1 (yrn, k2tog) to end.

Rows 4 and 5: K 1 row, then p 1 row.

Thread yarn through sts on needle, pull tight and secure by threading yarn a second time through sts.

MAKING UP

Note: Sew up all row-end seams on right side using mattress stitch one stitch in from the edge, unless otherwise stated; a one-stitch seam allowance has been allowed for this.

Slippers, legs, body and head

Sew up row ends of slippers and ankles. With markers at tips of toes, oversew cast-on stitches; leg seam will be ¼in (6mm) on inside edge of heel. Place a ball of stuffing into toes. Sew up row ends of legs and sew round crotch. Stuff legs, sew up row ends of body and head, and stuff body and head. Pull stitches on a thread tight at top of head and fasten off. To shape neck, take a double length of pale pink yarn and sew a running stitch round row with marker at neck, sewing in and out of every half stitch. Pull tight, knot yarn and sew ends into neck.

Skirt
Sew up row ends of skirt. Fold picot edge under and hem in place. Place skirt on doll and sew cast-off stitches of skirt to first row of upper body all the way round.

Sleeves, hands and sleeve frills
Sew up straight row ends of arms and sleeves from fingers to underarm and stuff arms using tweezers or tip of scissors. Leaving armholes open, sew arms to body, sewing top of arms to second row below neck at each side. Fold sleeve frills along picot edge and oversew cast-on and cast-off stitches. Place sleeve frills around arms and oversew row ends. Sew sleeve frills to sleeves all the way round.

Neck edging
Place neck edging around neck and oversew row ends. Pin neck edging around top of dress and over shoulders and sew in place using back stitch down centre of neck edging.

Features
Work features, as for Skateboarder on page 15.

Hair and hair loops
Make up hair, as for Valentine on page 23. Sew up row ends of hair loops and sew hair loops to hair, two at each side.

Wings
Fold cast-on stitches of wings in half and oversew. Oversew shaped row ends and stuff wings. Oversew straight row ends and sew two wings together down the middle. Sew wings to back of Fairy.

Wand
Cut chenille stem to length of stick. Place stick around chenille stem and sew up row ends along length, enclosing chenille stem inside. Gather round top and bottom of stick, pull tight and secure. Gather round cast-on stitches of head of wand, pull tight and secure. Fold head of wand along picot edge, place stick inside and sew along all row ends. Sew wand to hand of Fairy.

Bride & Groom

Materials

- ♥ Any DK (US: light worsted) yarn (amounts given are approximate):
  20g white (A)
  10g pale pink (B)
  5g brown (C)
  5g bright pink (D)
  5g black (E)
  5g dark grey (F)
  5g dark brown (G)
  5g silver grey (H)
- ♥ Oddments of black, red and pale green for embroidery
- ♥ 1 pair of 3.25mm (UK10:US3) needles and a spare needle of the same size and 1 pair of 4mm (UK8:US6) for veil for Bride only
- ♥ Knitters' pins and a blunt-ended needle for sewing up
- ♥ Tweezers (optional)
- ♥ Acrylic toy stuffing
- ♥ A red pencil for shading cheeks

Finished size

Bride stands 6in (15cm) tall
Groom stands 6³/₄in (17cm) tall

Tension

26 sts x 34 rows measure 4in (10cm) square over st-st using 3.25mm needles and DK yarn before stuffing

Abbreviations

See page 219

How to make Bride

SLIPPERS, LEGS, BODY AND HEAD
Right leg
Using the long tail method and A for slipper, cast on 14 sts.
Place a marker on cast-on edge between the 5th and 6th st of the sts just cast on.
Row 1 (WS): Purl.
Row 2: K2, (m1, k2) to end (20 sts).
Rows 3 and 4: P 1 row then k 1 row.
Row 5: Change to B for leg and p 1 row.

Row 6: K2, (k2tog) 6 times, k6 (14 sts).
Row 7: P7, p2tog, p1, p2tog, p2 (12 sts).
Rows 8 to 21: Work 14 rows in st-st. Break yarn and set aside.

Left leg
Using the long tail method and A for slipper, cast on 14 sts.
Place a marker on cast-on edge between the 9th and 10th st of the sts just cast on.
Row 1 (WS): Purl.
Row 2: K2, (m1, k2) to end (20 sts).

Rows 3 and 4: P 1 row then k 1 row.
Row 5: Change to B for leg and p 1 row.
Row 6: K6, (k2tog) 6 times, k2 (14 sts).
Row 7: P2, p2tog, p1, p2tog, p7 (12 sts).
Rows 8 to 21: Work 14 rows in st-st.

Join legs
Row 22: Change to A for lower body and with RS facing, k across sts of left leg then with the same yarn cont k across sts of right leg (24 sts).
Rows 23 to 27: Beg with a p row, work 5 rows in st-st.
Place a marker on last row for waist gathering.
Rows 28 to 33: Beg with a k row, work 6 rows in st-st.
Rows 34 to 37: Change to B for neck and work 4 rows in st-st.
Place a marker on last row for neck gathering.
Rows 38 and 39: Work 2 rows in st-st.
Row 40: K2, (m1, k4) to last 2 sts, m1, k2 (30 sts).
Rows 41 to 49: Beg with a p row, work 9 rows in st-st.
Row 50: (K2tog, k1) to end (20 sts).
Row 51: Purl.
Row 52: (K2tog) to end (10 sts).
Thread yarn through sts on needle and leave loose.

SKIRT
Using the long tail method and A, cast on 40 sts and beg in g-st, RS facing to beg.
Rows 1 and 2: Work 2 rows in g-st.
Rows 3 to 24: Beg with a k row, work 22 rows in st-st.
Row 25: (K2tog, k3) to end (32 sts).
Row 26: Purl.
Row 27: (K2tog, k2) to end (24 sts).
Cast off pwise.

ARMS AND HANDS

Make arms and hands in B, as for Ballerina on page 34.

NECK EDGING

Make neck edging in A, as for Fairy on page 41.

HAIR

Make hair in C, as for Valentine on page 22.

VEIL

Using the long tail method, 4mm needles and A, cast on 21 sts loosely, WS facing to beg.
Row 1: K1, (yf, k2tog) to end.

Rep row 1 until work measures 4½in (12cm), finishing with a WS row.
Change to 3.25mm needles and dec:
Next row: (K1, k2tog) to end (14 sts).
Next row: (P2tog) to end (7 sts).
Thread yarn through sts on needle, pull tight and secure by threading yarn a second time through sts.

ROSES (make 3 for top of veil and 7 for bouquet)

Using the long tail method and D, cast on 12 sts.
Row 1 (RS): (K2tog) to end (6 sts).
Thread yarn through sts on needle, pull tight and secure by threading yarn a second time through sts.

BOUQUET (make 2 pieces)

Using the long tail method and A, cast on 24 sts.
Row 1 (WS): Purl.
Row 2: (K2tog, k1) to end (16 sts).
Row 3: Purl.
Row 4: (K2tog) to end (8 sts).
Thread yarn through sts on needle, pull tight and secure by threading yarn a second time through sts.

MAKING UP

Note: Sew up all row-end seams on right side using mattress stitch one stitch in from the edge, unless otherwise stated; a one-stitch seam allowance has been allowed for this.

Slippers, legs, body and head

Sew up row ends of slippers and ankles. With markers at tips of toes, oversew cast-on stitches; leg seam will be ¼in (6mm) on inside edge of heel. Place a ball of stuffing into toes. Sew up row ends of legs and sew round crotch. Stuff legs, sew up row ends of body and head, and stuff body and head. Pull stitches on a thread tight at top of head and fasten off. To shape neck, take a double length of pale pink yarn and sew a running stitch round row with marker at neck, sewing in and out of every half stitch. Pull tight, knot yarn and sew ends into neck. To shape waist, take a double length of white yarn and sew a running stitch round row with marker at waist. Pull waist in, knot yarn and sew ends into waist.

Skirt

Sew up row ends of skirt. Place skirt on doll and sew cast-off stitches of skirt to waist all the way round.

Arms and hands

Make up arms and hands, as for Ballerina on page 35.

Neck edging

Make up neck edging, as for Fairy on page 43.

Features and hair

Work features, as for Skateboarder on page 15. Make up hair, as for Valentine on page 23.

Veil and roses

Sew stitches pulled tight on a thread of veil to top of head. Roll up roses and sew in place and sew three roses to front of veil.

Bouquet

Sew up row ends of both pieces of bouquet. Roll up roses and sew in place. Sew seven roses to one piece of bouquet. Embroider loops on bouquet in pale green. Sew back piece of bouquet to back of bouquet. Sew bouquet to hand of Bride.

How to make Groom

SHOES, LEGS, BODY AND HEAD

Make shoes, legs, body and head using E for shoes, B for legs, F for lower body, A for upper body and B for head, as for Skateboarder on page 13.

TROUSERS AND BELT

Make trousers and belt using F throughout, as for Cowboy on page 18.

ARMS AND HANDS

Make arms and hands in B, as for Skateboarder on pages 13 and 14.

HAIR

Using the long tail method and G, cast on 16 sts and work in g-st.
Row 1 (RS): Knit.
Row 2: K1, (m1, k2) to last st, m1, k1 (24 sts).
Rows 3 to 9: Work 7 rows in g-st, ending with a RS row.
Row 10: K1, m1, k to last st, m1, k1 (26 sts).

Row 11: Using the knitting-on method cast on 6 sts at beg of next row and k this row (32 sts).
Rows 12 to 14: Work 3 rows in g-st.
Row 15: (K2tog, k2) to end (24 sts).
Row 16 and foll alt row: Knit.
Row 17: (K2tog, k1) to end (16 sts).
Row 19: (K2tog) to end (8 sts).
Row 20: Knit.
Thread yarn through sts on needle, pull tight and secure by threading yarn a second time through sts.

TAILCOAT

Note: Sleeves are worked first and knitted into body.

Sleeves (make 2)

Beg at cuff using the long tail method and A, cast on 12 sts.
Row 1 (RS): Change to E and k 1 row.
Row 2: K3, (m1, k2) to last st, k1 (16 sts).
Rows 3 to 9: Beg with a k row, work 7 rows in st-st, finishing with a RS row.
Row 10: Cast off 3 sts pwise, p9, cast off rem 3 sts pwise and fasten off (10 sts).
Set aside.
Rep second sleeve as for first sleeve and set aside.

Left coat-tails

Using the long tail method and E, cast on 5 sts, WS facing to beg.
Row 1 and foll 4 alt rows: Purl.
Row 2: K3, (m1, k1) twice (7 sts).
Row 4: K5, (m1, k1) twice (9 sts).
Row 6: K7, (m1, k1) twice (11 sts).
Row 8: K9, (m1, k1) twice (13 sts).
Row 10: K11, (m1, k1) twice (15 sts).
Row 11: Purl.
Break yarn and set aside.

Right coat-tails

Using the long tail method and E, cast on 5 sts, WS facing to beg.
Row 1 and foll 4 alt rows: Purl.
Row 2: (K1, m1) twice, k3 (7 sts).
Row 4: (K1, m1) twice, k5 (9 sts).
Row 6: (K1, m1) twice, k7 (11 sts).
Row 8: (K1, m1) twice, k9 (13 sts).
Row 10: (K1, m1) twice, k11 (15 sts).
Row 11: Purl.

Join coat-tails

Row 12: With RS facing, K across right coat-tails then with the same yarn cont k across left coat-tails (30 sts.)

Row 13: K1, m1, p to last st, m1, k1 (32 sts).

Row 14: P2, k to last 2 sts, p2.

Row 15: K2, m1, p to last 2 sts, m1, k2 (34 sts).

Row 16: P3, k to last 3 sts, p3.

Divide for armholes

Row 17: K3, m1, p3, cast off 4 sts pwise, p13, cast off 4 sts pwise, p2, m1, k3 (28 sts).

Join sleeves

Row 18: With RS of all pieces facing, p4, k3 from right front, k10 from one sleeve, k14 across back, k10 from other sleeve, k3, p4 from left front (48 sts).

Row 19: K4, m1, p1, (p2tog) twice, p6, (p2tog) twice, p10, (p2tog) twice, p6, (p2tog) twice, p1, m1, k4 (42 sts).

Row 20: P4, k1, (k2tog) twice, k4, (k2tog) twice, k8, (k2tog) twice, k4, (k2tog) twice, k1, p4 (34 sts).

Row 21: K4, p to last 4 sts, k4.

Row 22: P4, (k2tog) twice, k2, (k2tog) twice, k6, (k2tog) twice, k2, (k2tog) twice, p4 (26 sts).

Row 23: K4, p to last 4 sts, k4.

Work collar

Rows 24 to 26: Beg with a p row, work 3 rows in st-st.
Cast off kwise.

BOW TIE

Using the long tail method and D, cast on 6 sts and work in g-st, RS facing to beg.

Rows 1 to 3: Work 3 rows in g-st.
Cast off in g-st.

TOP HAT

Using the long tail method and H, cast on 40 sts and beg in g-st, RS facing to beg.

Rows 1 and 2: Work 2 rows in g-st.
Change to F for hat band and dec:

Row 3: K1, (k2tog, k1) to end (27 sts).

Rows 4 and 5: P 1 row then k 1 row.

Rows 6 to 10: Cont in H and beg with a p row, work 5 rows in st-st.

Rows 11 and 12: P 2 rows for fold line.

Row 13: (K2tog, k1) to end (18 sts).
Row 14: Purl.
Row 15: (K2tog) to end (9 sts).
Thread yarn through sts on needle, pull tight and secure by threading yarn a second time through sts.

MAKING UP

Note: Sew up all row-end seams on right side using mattress stitch one stitch in from the edge, unless otherwise stated; a one-stitch seam allowance has been allowed for this.

Shoes, legs, body and head

Make up shoes, legs, body and head, as for Skateboarder on page 15.

Trousers and belt

Make up trousers and belt, as for Cowboy on page 19.

Arms, hands and features

Make up arms and hands and work features, as for Skateboarder on page 15.

Hair

Oversew row ends of hair from crown to side of forehead. Place hair on doll and sew in place using back stitch along outside edge.

Tailcoat

Sew up sleeve seams of coat-tails and sew across underarm. Place coat-tails on doll and turn collar back and sew in place.

Bow tie

To shape bow tie, wind matching yarn tightly around middle of bow and knot at back. Sew bow tie to front of neck.

Top hat

Sew up row ends of top hat and stuff top hat. Pin top hat to head and sew in place using back stitch at base of brim, sewing through hat to head all the way round.

Tennis Player

Materials

- Any DK (US: light worsted) yarn (amounts given are approximate):
  10g white (A)
  5g pale lime green (B)
  5g pale pink (C)
  5g brown (D)
  5g black (E)
  2g classic red (F)
  2g gold (G)
- Oddments of black, red, silver grey, beige and white for embroidery
- 1 pair of 3.25mm (UK10:US3) needles and a spare needle of the same size
- Knitters' pins and a blunt-ended needle for sewing up
- Tweezers (optional)
- Acrylic toy stuffing
- 2 chenille stems
- 1 plastic drinking straw (³/₁₆in/5mm diameter)
- A red pencil for shading cheeks

Finished size

Tennis Player stands 6in (15cm) tall

Tension

26 sts x 34 rows measure 4in (10cm) square over st-st using 3.25mm needles and DK yarn before stuffing

Abbreviations

See page 219

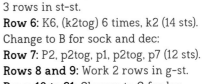

How to make Tennis Player

SHOES, SOCKS, LEGS, BODY AND HEAD
Right leg
Using the long tail method and A for shoe, cast on 14 sts.

Place a marker on cast-on edge between the 5th and 6th st of the sts just cast on.

Row 1 (WS): Purl.

Row 2: K2, (m1, k2) to end (20 sts).

Rows 3 to 5: Beg with a p row, work 3 rows in st-st.

Row 6: K2, (k2tog) 6 times, k6 (14 sts). Change to B for sock and dec:

Row 7: P7, p2tog, p1, p2tog, p2 (12 sts).

Rows 8 and 9: Work 2 rows in g-st.

Rows 10 to 21: Change to C for leg and beg with a k row, work 12 rows in st-st.

Break yarn and set aside.

Left leg
Using the long tail method and A for shoe, cast on 14 sts.

Place a marker on cast-on edge between the 9th and 10th st of the sts just cast on.

Row 1 (WS): Purl.

Row 2: K2, (m1, k2) to end (20 sts).

Rows 3 to 5: Beg with a p row, work 3 rows in st-st.

Row 6: K6, (k2tog) 6 times, k2 (14 sts). Change to B for sock and dec:

Row 7: P2, p2tog, p1, p2tog, p7 (12 sts).

Rows 8 and 9: Work 2 rows in g-st.

Rows 10 to 21: Change to C for leg and beg with a k row, work 12 rows in st-st.

Join legs
Row 22: Change to A for lower body and with RS facing, k across sts of left leg then with the same yarn cont k across sts of right leg (24 sts).

Rows 23 to 27: Beg with a p row, work 5 rows in st-st.

Rows 28 to 37: Change to C for upper body and work 10 rows in st-st. Place a marker on last row for neck gathering.

Rows 38 and 39: Work 2 rows in st-st.

Row 40: K2, (m1, k4) to last 2 sts, m1, k2 (30 sts).

Rows 41 to 49: Beg with a p row, work 9 rows in st-st.

Row 50: (K2tog, k1) to end (20 sts).

Row 51: Purl.

Row 52: (K2tog) to end (10 sts). Thread yarn through sts on needle and leave loose.

SHORTS
First leg
Beg at lower edge using the long tail method and A cast on 21 sts.

Row 1 (RS): Purl.

Rows 2 to 4: Beg with a p row, work 3 rows in st-st.

Rows 5 and 6: Cast off 2 sts at beg of next 2 rows (17 sts).

Break yarn and set aside.

Second leg
Work second leg as for first leg but do not break yarn.

Join legs

Row 7: With RS facing, k across sts of second leg then with the same yarn cont k across sts of first leg (34 sts).
Rows 8 to 12: Beg with a p row, work 5 rows in st-st.
Cast off.

ARMS AND HANDS

Make arms and hands in C, as for Ballerina on page 34.

HAIR

Make hair in D, as for Skateboarder on page 14.

T-SHIRT

Note: Sleeves are worked first and knitted into body.

Sleeves (make 2)

Using the long tail method and A, cast on 16 sts, RS facing to beg.
Rows 1 to 3: Beg with a k row, work 3 rows in st-st, finishing with a RS row.
Row 4: Cast off 3 sts pwise, p9, cast off rem 3 sts pwise and fasten off (10 sts).
Set aside.
Rep second sleeve as for first sleeve and set aside.

Front and back

Using the long tail method and A, cast on 38 sts, RS facing to beg.
Rows 1 to 7: Beg with a k row, work 7 rows in st-st finishing with a RS row.

Divide for armholes

Row 8: P8, cast off 4 sts pwise, p13, cast off 4 sts pwise, p7 (30 sts).

Join sleeves

Row 9: With RS of all pieces facing, k8 from left back, k10 from one sleeve, k14 across front, k10 from other sleeve, k8 from right back (50 sts).

Row 10: P6, (p2tog) twice, p6, (p2tog) twice, p10, (p2tog) twice, p6, (p2tog) twice, p6 (42 sts).
Row 11: K5, (k2tog) twice, k4, (k2tog) twice, k8, (k2tog) twice, k4, (k2tog) twice, k5 (34 sts).

Divide for front opening

Row 12: P16, k2, p16.

Work left back and left front

Row 13: K4, (k2tog) twice, k2, (k2tog) twice, k3, turn and work on these 13 sts.
Row 14: K1, p to end.
Row 15: K3, (k2tog, k3) twice (11 sts).

Work collar

Row 16: Knit.
Row 17: P3, (m1, p2) 3 times, m1, p1, k1 (15 sts).
Row 18: Knit.
Row 19: P to last st, k1.
Row 20: Knit.
Cast off kwise.

Work right front and right back

Row 21: Rejoin yarn to rem sts and K3, (k2tog) twice, k2, (k2tog) twice, k4 (13 sts).
Row 22: P to last st, k1.
Row 23: K3, (k2tog, k3) twice (11 sts).

Work collar

Row 24: Knit.
Row 25: K1, p1, (m1, p2) 3 times, m1, p3 (15 sts).
Row 26: Knit.
Row 27: K1, p to end.
Row 28: Knit.
Cast off kwise.

HEADBAND

Using the long tail method and A, cast on 50 sts.
Cast off kwise.

TENNIS RACKET AND BALL
Head of tennis racket
Using the long tail method and E, cast on 5 sts, WS facing to beg. Beg with a p row, work in st-st until piece measures 4in (10cm). Cast off.

Handle
Using the long tail method and F, cast on 7 sts and beg in g-st, RS facing to beg.
Rows 1 to 6: Work 6 rows in g-st.
Rows 7 to 12: Change to E and beg with a k row, work 6 rows in st-st. Cast off.

Ball
Using the long tail method and G, cast on 5 sts.
Row 1 (WS): Purl.
Row 2: K1, (m1, k1) to end (9 sts).
Rows 3 to 5: Beg with a p row, work 3 rows in st-st.
Row 6: (K2tog, k1) to end (6 sts). Thread yarn through sts on needle and leave loose.

MAKING UP
Note: Sew up all row-end seams on right side using mattress stitch one stitch in from the edge, unless otherwise stated; a one-stitch seam allowance has been allowed for this.

Shoes, legs, body and head
Sew up row ends of shoes. With markers at tips of toes, oversew cast-on stitches; leg seam will be ¼in (6mm) on inside edge of heel. Place a ball of stuffing into toes, sew up row ends of socks and legs and sew round crotch. Stuff legs, sew up row ends of body and head, and stuff body and head. Pull stitches on a thread tight at top of head and fasten off. To shape neck, take a double piece of pale pink yarn and sew a running stitch round row with marker on at neck, sewing in and out of every half stitch. Pull tight, knot yarn and sew ends into neck.

Shorts
Sew up leg seams of shorts and sew round crotch. Sew up row ends at centre back and place shorts on doll. Sew cast-off stitches of shorts to first row of upper body all the way round.

Arms and hands
Make up arms and hands, as for Ballerina on page 35.

Features, hair and embroidery
Work features and make up hair, as for Skateboarder on page 15. Using picture as a guide, embroider lines on shoes in silver grey using straight stitches.

T-shirt
Sew up sleeve seams of t-shirt and sew across under arm. Place t-shirt on doll and sew up back seam and row ends of collar. Fold collar down and sew in place.

Headband
Pin headband around head and sew together ½in (13mm) from row ends. Using back stitch sew around headband, sewing through headband to head.

Tennis racket and ball
Place two chenille stems together and cut to 6in (15cm) long. Place head of tennis racket around chenille stems at centre and sew up row ends, enclosing chenille sticks inside (1in [2.5cm] of chenille stem will be showing at both ends). Curve chenille stems around, bringing points together, push into a piece of plastic drinking straw cut to 1¼in (3cm). Shape head of tennis racket into an oval. Gather round cast-on stitches of handle, pull tight and secure. Place handle around straw and sew up row ends along length, enclosing straw inside, and sew cast-off stitches of handle to head of tennis racket where they meet. Embroider strings using beige. Sew up row ends of ball and stuff using tweezers or tip of scissors. Pull stitches on a thread tight and secure. Embroider a wavy white line on ball using back stitch. Sew tennis racket and ball to hand of doll.

Pirate

Materials

- ♥ Any DK (US: light worsted) yarn (amounts given are approximate):
  5g black (A)
  5g pale pink (B)
  5g white (C)
  5g red (D)
  5g royal blue (E)
  5g pale brown (F)
  5g brown (G)
  5g purple (H)
  2g gold (I)
  2g lemon (J)
  2g pale blue (K)
  2g dark grey (L)
  5g silver grey (M)
- ♥ Oddments of black, red, gold and white for embroidery
- ♥ 1 pair of 3.25mm (UK10:US3) needles and a spare needle of the same size
- ♥ Knitters' pins and a blunt-ended needle for sewing up
- ♥ Tweezers (optional)
- ♥ Acrylic toy stuffing
- ♥ Small piece of thick cardboard
- ♥ A red pencil for shading cheeks

Finished size

Pirate stands 6³/₄in (17cm) tall

Tension

26 sts x 34 rows measure 4in (10cm) square over st-st using 3.25mm needles and DK yarn before stuffing

Abbreviations

See page 219

How to make Pirate

BOOTS, LEGS, BODY AND HEAD
Right leg
Using the long tail method and A for boot, cast on 14 sts.
Place a marker on cast-on edge between the 5th and 6th st of the sts just cast on.
Row 1 (WS): Purl.
Row 2: K2, (m1, k2) to end (20 sts).
Rows 3 to 5: Beg with a p row, work 3 rows in st-st.
Row 6: K2, (k2tog) 6 times, k6 (14 sts).
Row 7: P7, p2tog, p1, p2tog, p2 (12 sts).
Rows 8 to 21: Change to B for leg and work 14 rows in st-st.
Break yarn and set aside.

Left leg
Using the long tail method and A for boot, cast on 14 sts.
Place a marker on cast-on edge between the 9th and 10th st of the sts just cast on.
Row 1 (WS): Purl.
Row 2: K2, (m1, k2) to end (20 sts).
Rows 3 to 5: Beg with a p row, work 3 rows in st-st.
Row 6: K6, (k2tog) 6 times, k2 (14 sts).
Row 7: P2, p2tog, p1, p2tog, p7 (12 sts).
Rows 8 to 21: Change to B for leg and work 14 rows in st-st.

Join legs
Row 22: Change to C for lower body and with RS facing, k across sts of left leg then with the same yarn cont k across sts of right leg (24 sts).
Rows 23 to 27: Beg with a p row, work 5 rows in st-st.
Rows 28 to 37: Join on D for upper body and work 10 rows in st-st in stripes, 2 rows D then 2 rows C and rep this ending with 2 rows D.
Rows 38 and 39: Change to B for head and work 2 rows in st-st.
Row 40: K2, (m1, k4) to last 2 sts, m1, k2 (30 sts).
Rows 41 to 49: Beg with a p row, work 9 rows in st-st.
Row 50: (K2tog, k1) to end (20 sts).
Row 51: Purl.
Row 52: (K2tog) to end (10 sts).
Thread yarn through sts on needle and leave loose.

BREECHES
First leg
Beg at lower edge using the long tail method and E, cast on 21 sts.
Row 1 (RS): Purl.
Rows 2 to 8: Beg with a p row, work 7 rows in st-st.
Rows 9 and 10: Cast off 2 sts at beg of next 2 rows (17 sts).
Break yarn and set aside.

Second leg
Work second leg as for first leg but do not break yarn.

Join legs
Row 11: With RS facing, k across sts of second leg then with the same yarn cont k across sts of first leg (34 sts).
Rows 12 to 14: Beg with a p row, work 3 rows in st-st.
Rows 15 and 16: Change to F for belt and work 2 rows in g-st.
Cast off pwise.

BOOT TOPS (make 2)

Using the long tail method and A, cast on 20 sts, WS facing to beg. Cast off kwise.

SLEEVES AND HANDS (make 2)

Beg at shoulder using the long tail method and C, cast on 5 sts.
Row 1 (WS): Purl.
Join on D and work 6 rows in st-st in stripes, 2 rows D then 2 rows C and repeat this ending with 2 rows C and AT THE SAME TIME shape:
Row 2: K1, (m1, k1) to end (9 sts).
Row 3: Purl.
Row 4: K1, m1, k to last st, m1, k1 (11 sts).
Rows 5 and 6: Rep rows 3 and 4 once (13 sts).
Row 7: Using D, purl.
Rows 8 to 13: Work 6 rows in st-st in stripes as set.
Change to B for hand and dec:
Row 14: K3, (k2tog, k3) twice (11 sts).

Rows 15 to 17: Beg with a p row, work 3 rows in st-st.
Row 18: K2tog, (k1, k2tog) to end (7 sts).
Thread yarn through sts on needle, pull tight and secure by threading yarn a second time through sts.

CUFFS

Make cuffs in C, as for Cowboy on page 18.

HAIR

Make hair in G, as for Skateboarder on page 14.

NECKERCHIEF

Make neckerchief in H, as for Cowboy on page 18.

THREE-CORNERED HAT

Using the long tail method and I, cast on 56 sts.
Row 1 (RS): Change to A and k 1 row.
Row 2: P8, (p2tog) 4 times, p8, (p2tog) 4 times, p1, turn.
Row 3: S1k, k5, turn.
Row 4: S1p, (p2tog) twice, p2, turn.
Row 5: S1k, k5, turn.
Row 6: S1p, p11, (p2tog) 4 times, p8 (42 sts).
Row 7: Knit.
Row 8: P8, p3tog, p8, (p2tog) twice, p8, p3tog, p8 (36 sts).
Rows 9 and 10: Work 2 rows in g-st for fold line.
Rows 11 and 12: K 1 row then p 1 row.

Work crown

Rows 13 to 17: Beg with a p row, work 5 rows in st-st.
Row 18: (K2tog, k2) to end (27 sts).
Row 19 and foll alt row: Purl.
Row 20: (K2tog, k1) to end (18 sts)
Row 22: (K2tog) to end (9 sts).
Thread yarn through sts on needle, pull tight and secure by threading yarn a second time through sts.

PATCHES
(make 2: 1 in J and 1 in K)
Using the long tail method and J or K, cast on 4 sts and work in g-st, RS facing to beg.

Rows 1 to 3: Work 3 rows in g-st.

Cast off in g-st.

SWORD
Handle
Using the long tail method and L, cast on 7 sts and work in rev st-st, RS facing to beg.

Rows 1 to 5: Beg with a p row, work 5 rows in rev st-st.

Cast off.

Blade
Using the long tail method and M, cast on 16 sts, WS facing to beg.

Row 1: P12, turn.

Row 2: S1k, k7, turn.

Row 3: S1p, p to end.

Row 4: K2, (k2tog, k2) 3 times, turn.

Row 5: S1p, p to end (13 sts).

Row 6: (K3, m1) 3 times, k3, turn.

Row 7: S1p, p to end.

Row 8: K12, turn.

Row 9: S1p, p7, turn.

Row 10: S1k, k to end.

Cast off pwise.

MAKING UP
Note: Sew up all row-end seams on right side using mattress stitch one stitch in from the edge, unless otherwise stated; a one-stitch seam allowance has been allowed for this.

Boots, legs, body and head
Make up boots, legs, body and head, as for Cowboy on page 19.

Breeches
Sew up leg seams of breeches and sew round crotch. Sew up row ends at centre back and place breeches on doll. Sew cast-off stitches of breeches to first row of upper body all the way round.

Boot tops
Place boot tops around boots and sew up at back. Sew boot tops to top of boots all the way round.

Sleeves, hands and cuffs
Make up sleeves, hands and cuffs, as for Cowboy on page 19.

Features and hair
Work features and make up hair, as for Skateboarder on page 15.

Neckerchief
Make up neckerchief, as for Cowboy on page 19.

Three-cornered hat
Using gold, oversew wrong side of gold edging, catching together lower loop of cast-on edge and last loop of knitting along this edge. Sew up row ends of hat and fold brim up. Pin hat to head and sew to head all the way round.

Patches and embroidery
Using picture as a guide, sew patches to breeches and embroider stitches in black. Embroider buckle on breeches in gold, making four double stitches. Embroider skull and crossbones on front of hat in white.

Sword
Sew up row ends of handle of sword and stuff using tweezers or tip of scissors. Fold blade, bringing cast-on and cast-off stitches together, and place on piece of thick cardboard. Draw around shape and cut out shape inside the line. Place knitting around cardboard shape and sew up cast-on and cast-off stitches, enclosing cardboard inside. Sew blade to handle of sword and sew sword to hand of Pirate.

Doctor

Materials

- ♥ Any DK (US: light worsted) yarn (amounts given are approximate):
  5g dark brown (A)
  5g pale pink (B)
  5g silver grey (C)
  10g white (D)
  5g medium brown (E)
  2g red (F)
  5g black (G)
  2g dark grey (H)
- ♥ Oddments of black, red and dark grey for embroidery
- ♥ 1 pair of 3.25mm (UK10:US3) needles and a spare needle of the same size
- ♥ Knitters' pins and a blunt-ended needle for sewing up
- ♥ Tweezers (optional)
- ♥ Acrylic toy stuffing
- ♥ 1 chenille stem
- ♥ A red pencil for shading cheeks

Finished size

Doctor stands 6in (15cm) tall

Tension

26 sts x 34 rows measure 4in (10cm) square over st-st using 3.25mm needles and DK yarn before stuffing

Abbreviations

See page 219

How to make Doctor

SHOES, LEGS, BODY, HEAD AND TROUSERS

Make shoes, legs, body, head and trousers using A for shoes, B for legs, C for lower body, D for upper body, B for head and make trousers in E, as for Skateboarder on page 13.

SLEEVES AND HANDS (make 2)

Beg at shoulder using the long tail method and D, cast on 4 sts.
Row 1 (WS): Purl.
Row 2: K1, (m1, k1) to end (7 sts).
Row 3: Purl.
Row 4: K1, m1, k to last st, m1, k1 (9 sts).
Rows 5 and 6: Rep rows 3 and 4 once (11 sts).

Rows 7 to 14: Beg with a p row, work 8 rows in st-st, finishing with a RS row.
Rows 15 to 17: Change to B for hand and beg with a p row, work 3 rows in st-st.
Row 18: K2tog, (k1, k2tog) to end (7 sts).
Thread yarn through sts on needle, pull tight and secure by threading yarn a second time through sts.

TIE

Using the long tail method and F, cast on 10 sts.
Cast off pwise.

HAIR

Make hair in G, as for Groom on page 48.

WHITE COAT

Note: Sleeves are worked first and knitted into body.

Sleeves (make 2)

Beg at cuff using the long tail method and D, cast on 16 sts and beg in g-st, RS facing to beg.
Rows 1 and 2: Work 2 rows in g-st.
Rows 3 to 9: Beg with a k row, work 7 rows in st-st, finishing with a RS row.
Row 10: Cast off 3 sts pwise, p9, cast off rem 3 sts pwise and fasten off (10 sts).
Set aside.
Rep second sleeve as for first sleeve and set aside.

Front and back

Using the long tail method and D, cast on 46 sts and beg in g-st, RS facing to beg.
Rows 1 and 2: Work 2 rows in g-st.
Row 3: Knit.
Row 4: K2, p to last 2 sts, k2.
Rows 5 to 10: Rep rows 3 and 4, 3 times more.
Row 11: *K8, k2tog, k3, k2tog, k8; rep from * once (42 sts).
Rows 12 to 16: Rep row 4 once, then rep rows 3 and 4 twice more.
Row 17: *K7, k2tog, k3, k2tog, k7; rep from * once (38 sts).

Divide for armholes

Row 18: K2, p6, cast off 4 sts pwise, p13, cast off 4 sts pwise, p5, k2 (30 sts).

Join sleeves

Row 19: With RS of all pieces facing, k8 from right front, k10 from one sleeve, k14 across back, k10 from other sleeve, k8 from left front (50 sts).

Row 20: K2, p4, (p2tog) twice, p6, (p2tog) twice, p10, (p2tog) twice, p6, (p2tog) twice, p4, k2 (42 sts).
Row 21: K1, p2, k2, (k2tog) twice, k4, (k2tog) twice, k8, (k2tog) twice, k4, (k2tog) twice, k2, p2, k1 (34 sts).
Row 22: K3, p to last 3 sts, k3.
Row 23: K1, p3, (k2tog) twice, k2, (k2tog) twice, k6, (k2tog) twice, k2, (k2tog) twice, p3, k1 (26 sts).
Row 24: K4, p to last 4 sts, k4.

Work collar
Row 25: K1, p to last st, k1.
Row 26: Knit.
Rows 27 and 28: Rep rows 25 and 26 once.
Cast off kwise.

STETHOSCOPE
Neck cord
Using the long tail method and C, cast on 5 sts, WS facing to beg.
Rows 1 to 7: Beg with a p row, work 7 rows in st-st.
Rows 8 to 23: Change to H and work 16 rows in st-st.
Rows 24 to 31: Change to C and work 8 rows in st-st.
Thread yarn through sts on needle, pull tight and secure by threading yarn a second time through sts.

Connector cord
Using the long tail method and H, cast on 5 sts, WS facing to beg.
Rows 1 to 9: Beg with a p row, work 9 rows in st-st.
Cast off.

Listening bell
(make 2 pieces)
Using the long tail method and C, cast on 10 sts.
Row 1 (RS): Knit.
Thread yarn through sts on needle, pull tight and secure by threading yarn a second time through sts.

MAKING UP

Note: Sew up all row-end seams on right side using mattress stitch one stitch in from the edge, unless otherwise stated; a one-stitch seam allowance has been allowed for this.

Shoes, legs, body, head and trousers

Make up shoes, legs, body, head and trousers, as for Skateboarder on page 15.

Sleeves and hands

Sew up straight row ends of sleeves from fingers to underarm and stuff arms using tweezers or tip of scissors. Leaving armholes open, sew arms to body, sewing top of arms to second row below neck at each side.

Tie

Fold over two stitches at one end of tie for knot of tie and stitch in place. Tie a tight thread around base of these stitches to shape knot of tie using matching yarn. Sew tie to body at centre front.

Features and hair

Work features, as for Skateboarder on page 15. Make up hair, as for Groom on page 51.

White coat

Sew up sleeve seams of white coat and sew across under arm. Place white coat on doll and fold collar back. Sew together down front of white coat. Embroider buttons down white coat in dark grey, making two small stitches close together for each button.

Stethoscope

Cut a piece of chenille stem to length of neck cord and oversew row ends of neck cord around chenille stem, enclosing chenille stem inside. Repeat for connector cord. Sew end of connector cord to middle of neck cord and bend neck cord into a 'U' shape and bend ¼in (6mm) of ends of neck cord in. Place two pieces of listening bell together, matching all edges, and oversew around outside edge. Sew listening bell to end of connector cord. Sew stethoscope to Doctor.

Nurse

Materials

- ♥ Any DK (US: light worsted) yarn (amounts given are approximate):
  5g white (A)
  5g pale pink (B)
  10g blue (C)
  5g red (D)
  5g brown (E)
- ♥ Oddments of black, red and silver grey for embroidery
- ♥ 1 pair of 3.25mm (UK10:US3) needles and a spare needle of the same size
- ♥ Knitters' pins and a blunt-ended needle for sewing up
- ♥ Tweezers (optional)
- ♥ Acrylic toy stuffing
- ♥ A red pencil for shading cheeks

Finished size

Nurse stands 6¼in (16cm) tall

Tension

26 sts x 34 rows measure 4in (10cm) square over st-st using 3.25mm needles and DK yarn before stuffing

Abbreviations

See page 219

How to make Nurse

SHOES, LEGS, BODY AND HEAD
Right leg
Using the long tail method and A for shoe, cast on 14 sts.
Place a marker on cast-on edge between the 5th and 6th st of the sts just cast on.
Row 1 (WS): Purl.
Row 2: K2, (m1, k2) to end (20 sts).
Rows 3 to 5: Beg with a p row, work 3 rows in st-st.
Row 6: K2, (k2tog) 6 times, k6 (14 sts). Change to B for leg and dec:
Row 7: P7, p2tog, p1, p2tog, p2 (12 sts).
Rows 8 to 21: Work 14 rows in st-st.
Break yarn and set aside.

Left leg
Using the long tail method and A for shoe, cast on 14 sts.
Place a marker on cast-on edge between the 9th and 10th st of the sts just cast on.
Row 1 (WS): Purl.
Row 2: K2, (m1, k2) to end (20 sts).
Rows 3 to 5: Beg with a p row, work 3 rows in st-st.
Row 6: K6, (k2tog) 6 times, k2 (14 sts). Change to B for leg and dec:
Row 7: P2, p2tog, p1, p2tog, p7 (12 sts).
Rows 8 to 21: Work 14 rows in st-st.

Join legs
Row 22: Change to A for lower body and with RS facing, k across sts of left leg then with the same yarn cont k across sts of right leg (24 sts).
Rows 23 to 27: Beg with a p row, work 5 rows in st-st.
Rows 28 to 37: Change to C for upper body and work 10 rows in st-st.
Rows 38 and 39: Change to B for head and work 2 rows in st-st.
Row 40: K2, (m1, k4) to last 2 sts, m1, k2 (30 sts).

Rows 41 to 49: Beg with a p row, work 9 rows in st-st.
Row 50: (K2tog, k1) to end (20 sts).
Row 51: Purl.
Row 52: (K2tog) to end (10 sts).
Thread yarn through sts on needle and leave loose.

SKIRT AND BELT
Using the long tail method and C, cast on 40 sts and beg in g-st, RS facing to beg.
Rows 1 and 2: Work 2 rows in g-st.
Rows 3 to 12: Beg with a k row, work 10 rows in st-st.
Change to D for belt and dec:
Row 13: (K2tog, k2) to end (30 sts).
Row 14: Knit.
Cast off pwise.

SLEEVES, ARMS, HANDS AND ARM CUFFS
Make sleeves, arms, hands and arm cuffs using C for sleeves and B for arms and hands and arm cuffs in A, as for Painter & Decorator on page 29.

HAIR
Make hair in E, as for Valentine on page 22.

COLLAR
Using the long tail method and A, cast on 26 sts.
Row 1 (RS): K 1 row.
Cast off kwise.

APRON
Using the long tail method and A, cast on 12 sts and beg in g-st, RS facing to beg.

Rows 1 and 2: Work 2 rows in g-st.
Row 3: Knit.
Row 4: K2, p to last 2 sts, k2.
Rows 5 to 8: Rep rows 3 and 4 twice more.
Row 9: K1, (k2tog, k2) twice, k2tog, k1 (9 sts).
Cast off pwise.

Bib

Beg at top edge using the long tail method and A, cast on 6 sts.
Row 1 (RS): Knit.
Row 2: K1, p to last st, k1.
Rows 3 and 4: Rep rows 1 and 2 once.
Cast off kwise.

CAP

Using the long tail method and A, cast on 30 sts, RS facing to beg.
Rows 1 to 5: Beg with a k row, work 5 rows in st-st, finishing with a RS row.
Row 6: Cast off 9 sts kwise, p11, cast off 9 sts kwise and fasten off.
Row 7: Rejoin yarn to rem sts and k to end (12 sts).
Row 8: Purl.
Row 9: K2tog, k to last 2 sts, k2tog (10 sts).
Rows 10 to 12: Beg with a p row, work 3 rows in st-st.
Rows 13 to 16: Rep rows 9 to 12 once (8 sts).
Row 17: As row 9 (6 sts).
Row 18: Purl.
Row 19: (K2tog) to end (3 sts).
Row 20: P3tog tbl and fasten off.

FOB WATCH

Using the long tail method and A, cast on 12 sts, RS facing to beg. Thread yarn through sts on needle, pull tight and secure by threading yarn a second time through sts.

MAKING UP

Note: Sew up all row-end seams on right side using mattress stitch one stitch in from the edge, unless otherwise stated; a one-stitch seam allowance has been allowed for this.

Shoes, legs, body and head

Make up shoes, legs, body and head, as for Skateboarder on page 15.

Skirt and belt

Sew up row ends of skirt and belt and place on doll. Sew belt to first row of upper body all the way round.

Sleeves, arms, hands and arm cuffs

Make up sleeves, arms, hands and arm cuffs, as for Painter & Decorator on page 31.

Features and hair

Work features, as for Skateboarder on page 15. Make up hair, as for Valentine on page 23.

Collar

Place collar around neck and sew together under chin. Sew collar to neck all the way round.

Apron

Place apron and apron bib on doll and sew all edges down.

Cap

Sew up row ends of wide part of cap and place on head. Sew lower edge to head all the way round. Fold point of triangle to back and stitch in place.

Fob watch and embroidery

Sew up row ends of fob watch and sew to chest. Embroider two lines for hands of clock in black. Embroider buckle on belt in silver grey, making eight vertical stitches close together at centre front. Embroider cross in red on cap, making double stitches.

Gardener

Materials

- ♥ Any DK (US: light worsted) yarn (amounts given are approximate):
  5g navy blue (A)
  5g pale pink (B)
  5g grey (C)
  5g buttermilk (D)
  5g green (E)
  5g brown (F)
  5g pale brown (G)
  2g orange (H)
- ♥ Oddments of black, red and bright green for embroidery
- ♥ 1 pair of 3.25mm (UK10:US3) needles and a spare needle of the same size
- ♥ Knitters' pins and a blunt-ended needle for sewing up
- ♥ Tweezers (optional)
- ♥ Acrylic toy stuffing
- ♥ A red pencil for shading cheeks

Finished size

Gardener stands 6in (15cm) tall

Tension

26 sts x 34 rows measure 4in (10cm) square over st-st using 3.25mm needles and DK yarn before stuffing

Abbreviations

See page 219

How to make Gardener

BOOTS, LEGS, BODY AND HEAD
Make boots, legs, body and head using A for boots, B for legs, C for lower body, D for upper body and B for head, as for Cowboy on page 17.

SLEEVES, ARMS, HANDS AND ARM CUFFS
Make sleeves, arms, hands and arm cuffs using D for sleeves, B for arms and hands and D for arm cuffs, as for Painter & Decorator on page 29.

COLLAR
Make collar in D, as for Nurse on page 65.

DUNGAREES
Make dungarees in E, as for Painter & Decorator on page 30.

HAIR
Make hair in F, as for Skateboarder on page 14.

CAP
Make cap in G, as for Painter & Decorator on page 30.

BUCKET
Beg at base using the long tail method and C, cast on 7 sts.
Row 1 (WS): Purl.
Row 2: (Kfb) to end (14 sts).
Rows 3 and 4: Work 2 rows in g-st.
Row 5: Purl.
Row 6: K5, m1, k4, m1, k5 (16 sts).
Rows 7 to 9: Beg with a p row, work 3 rows in st-st.
Rows 10 to 12: Work 3 rows in g-st.
Row 13: Purl.
Row 14: (K2tog) to end (8 sts).
Row 15: (P2tog) to end (4 sts).
Thread yarn through sts on needle, pull tight and secure by threading yarn a second time through sts.

69

Rim
Using the long tail method and C, cast on 25 sts.
Row 1 (RS): Knit.
Cast off kwise.

Handle
Using the long tail method and C, cast on 12 sts, WS facing to beg.
Rows 1 to 3: Beg with a p row, work 3 rows in st-st.
Cast off.

CARROTS (make 2)
Using the long tail method and H, cast on 9 sts, WS facing to beg.
Rows 1 to 3: Beg with a p row, work 3 rows in st-st.
Row 4: K2, k2tog, k1, k2tog, k2 (7 sts).
Row 5 and foll alt row: Purl.
Row 6: K1, (k2tog, k1) twice (5 sts).
Row 8: K2tog, k1, k2tog (3 sts).
Thread yarn through sts on needle, pull tight and secure by threading yarn a second time through sts.

MAKING UP
Note: Sew up all row-end seams on right side using mattress stitch one stitch in from the edge, unless otherwise stated; a one-stitch seam allowance has been allowed for this.

Boots, legs, body and head
Make up boots, legs, body and head, as for Cowboy on page 19.

Sleeves, arms, hands and arm cuffs

Make up sleeves, arms, hands and arm cuffs, as for Painter & Decorator on page 31.

Collar

Make up collar, as for Nurse on page 67.

Dungarees

Make up dungarees, as for Painter & Decorator on page 31.

Features and hair

Work features and make up hair, as for Skateboarder on page 15.

Cap

Make up cap, as for Painter & Decorator on page 31.

Bucket

Gather round cast-on stitches of bucket, pull tight and secure. Sew up row ends of top and bottom of bucket and stuff bucket. Sew up remaining row ends. Place rim around top of bucket and oversew row ends. Sew lower edge of rim to

top of bucket all the way round. Oversew cast-on and cast-off stitches of handle along length and sew ends of handle to either side of bucket. Sew bucket to hand of Gardener.

Carrots

Sew up row ends of carrots and stuff with a tiny amount of stuffing using tweezers or tip of scissors. Gather round cast-on stitches, pull tight and secure. Embroider loops in bright green at top of each carrot and secure with a double stitch. Sew carrots to hand of Gardener.

Union Jack Doll

Materials

- ♥ Any DK (US: light worsted) yarn (amounts given are approximate):
  15g red (A)
  5g pale pink (B)
  10g white (C)
  15g royal blue (D)
  5g dark brown (E)
  5g brown (F)
- ♥ Oddments of black and red for embroidery
- ♥ 1 pair of 3.25mm (UK10:US3) needles and a spare needle of the same size
- ♥ Knitters' blunt-ended pins and a needle for sewing up
- ♥ Tweezers (optional)
- ♥ Acrylic toy stuffing
- ♥ A red pencil for shading cheeks
- ♥ Wooden dowelling ¼in (6mm) in thickness, 7in (18cm long)

Finished size

Union Jack Doll stands 6¾in (17cm) tall

Tension

26 sts x 34 rows measure 4in (10cm) square over st-st using 3.25mm needles and DK yarn before stuffing

Abbreviations

See page 219

How to make Union Jack Doll

SHOES, LEGS, BODY, HEAD, TROUSERS, ARMS, HANDS AND HAIR

Make shoes, legs, body, head, trousers, arms, hands and hair using A for shoes, B for legs, C for lower body, A for upper body and B for head, trousers in D arms and hands in B and hair in E, as for Skateboarder on pages 13 and 14.

JUMPER

Note: Sleeves are worked first and knitted into body.

Sleeves (make 2)

Beg at cuff using the long tail method and A, cast on 16 sts, RS facing to beg.
Rows 1 and 2: P 1 row then k 1 row.
Rows 3 and 4: Join on C and k 1 row then p 1 row.
Rows 5 and 6: Join on D and k 1 row then p 1 row.
Work in stripes carrying yarn loosely up side of work:
Rows 7 and 8: Using A, k 1 row then p 1 row.
Rows 9 and 10: Using C, k 1 row then p 1 row.
Row 11: Using D, knit.
Row 12: Using D, cast off 3 sts pwise, p9, cast off rem 3 sts pwise and fasten off (10 sts).
Set aside.
Rep second sleeve as for first sleeve and set aside.

Front and back

Using the long tail method and A, cast on 38 sts, RS facing to beg.
Rows 1 and 2: P 1 row then k 1 row.
Rows 3 and 4: Join on C and k 1 row then p 1 row.
Rows 5 and 6: Join on D and k 1 row then p 1 row.

Work in stripes carrying yarn loosely up side of work:
Rows 7 and 8: Using A, k 1 row then p 1 row.
Rows 9 and 10: Using C, k 1 row then p 1 row.
Row 11: Using D, knit.

Divide for armholes

Row 12: Using D, p8, cast off 4 sts pwise, p13, cast off 4 sts pwise, p7 (30 sts).

Join sleeves

Row 13: Using A and with RS of all pieces facing, k8 from left back, k10 from one sleeve, k14 across front, k10 from other sleeve, k8 from right back (50 sts).
Row 14: Using A, P6, (p2tog) twice, p6, (p2tog) twice, p10, (p2tog) twice, p6, (p2tog) twice, p6 (42 sts).

Row 15: Using C, k5, (k2tog) twice, k4, (k2tog) twice, k8, (k2tog) twice, k4, (k2tog) twice, k5 (34 sts).
Row 16: Using C, purl.
Row 17: Using D, k4, (k2tog) twice, k2, (k2tog) twice, k6, (k2tog) twice, k2, (k2tog) twice, k4 (26 sts).
Row 18: Using D, purl.
Rows 19 and 20: Using A, work 2 rows in g-st.
Cast off pwise using A.

TOP HAT

Using the long tail method and A, cast on 40 sts and beg in g-st, RS facing to beg.
Rows 1 and 2: Work 2 rows in g-st.
Join on C and dec:
Row 3: K1, (k2tog, k1) to end (27 sts).
Rows 4 to 6: Beg with a p row, work 3 rows in st-st.

Rows 7 to 14: Cont in A and work 8 rows in st-st.
Rows 15 and 16: P 2 row for fold line.
Row 17: (K2tog, k1) to end (18 sts).
Row 18: Purl.
Row 19: (K2tog) to end (9 sts).
Thread yarn through sts on needle, pull tight and secure by threading yarn a second time through sts.

FLAG (make 2 pieces)

Beg at lower edge using the long tail method and C, cast on 32 sts. Join on A and D as required and work in A, C and D in Fair Isle from chart, reading RS rows from right to left and WS rows from left to right and place foundation row as foll:
Row 1 (WS): C-p2, A-p2, C-p1, D-p8, C-p1. A-p4, C-p1, D-p8, C-p3, A-p2.
Cont from row 2 of chart to row 25.
Cast off in C.

Pole

Using the long tail method and F, cast on 6 sts, WS facing to beg.
Beg with a p row, work in st-st for 7½in (19cm).
Cast off.

MAKING UP

Note: Sew up all row-end seams on right side using mattress stitch one stitch in from the edge, unless otherwise stated; a one-stitch seam allowance has been allowed for this.

Shoes, legs, body, head, trousers, arms, hands, features and hair

Make up shoes, legs, body, head, trousers, arms, hands, work features and make up hair, as for Skateboarder on page 15.

Jumper

Sew up sleeve seams of jumper and sew across under arm. Place jumper on doll and sew up back seam.

Top hat

Sew up row ends of top hat and stuff top hat. Pin top hat to head and sew in place using back stitch at base of brim sewing through hat to head all the way round.

Flag

Place wrong side of two pieces of flag together matching all edges and sew up outside edge. Cut dowelling to 7in (18cm) and place pole around piece of dowelling and oversew row ends along length, enclosing dowelling inside. Gather round cast-on and cast-off stitches of pole, pull tight and secure. Sew flag to pole and pole to hand of doll.

Lord of the Manor

Materials

- ♥ Any DK (US: light worsted) yarn (amounts given are approximate):
  5g dark brown (A)
  5g buttermilk (B)
  5g white (C)
  5g khaki green (D)
  5g pale pink (E)
  5g bottle green (F)
  5g mustard (G)
  2g lemon (H)
  5g ginger (I)
  5g brown (J)
- ♥ Oddments of black and red for embroidery and bottle green for making up
- ♥ 1 pair of 3.25mm (UK10:US3) needles and a spare needle of the same size
- ♥ Knitters' pins and a blunt-ended needle for sewing up
- ♥ Tweezers (optional)
- ♥ Acrylic toy stuffing
- ♥ A red pencil for shading cheeks
- ♥ 1 plastic drinking straw (3/16in/5mm diameter)

Finished size

Lord of the Manor stands 6¼in (16cm) tall

Tension

26 sts x 34 rows measure 4in (10cm) square over st-st using 3.25mm needles and DK yarn before stuffing

Abbreviations

See page 219

How to make Lord of the Manor

SHOES, LEGS, BODY AND HEAD

Make shoes, legs, body and head using A for shoes, B for legs, C for lower body, D for upper body and E for head, as for Nurse on page 65.

BREECHES

First leg

Beg at lower edge using the long tail method and F, cast on 20 sts.
Row 1 (RS): Knit.
Row 2: K5, (m1, k5) to end (23 sts).
Join on G and work in patt:
Row 3: Using G, k1, (s1p, k1) to end.
Row 4: Using G, k1, (yf, s1p, yb, k1) to end.
Rows 5 and 6: Using F, work 2 rows in g-st.
Rows 7 to 10: Rep rows 3 to 6 once.
Row 11: Using G, cast off 2 sts, (s1p, k1) to end (21 sts).
Row 12: Using G, cast off 2 sts pwise, s1p, yb, k1, (yf, s1p, yb, k1) to end (19 sts).
Break yarn and set aside.

Second leg

Work second leg as for first leg but do not break yarn.

Join legs

Row 13: With RS facing, rejoin F and k across sts of second leg then with the same yarn cont k across sts of first leg (38 sts).
Row 14: K19, m1, k19 (39 sts).
Rows 15 to 22: Rep rows 3 to 6 twice more.
Cont in F and dec:
Row 23: K5, (k2tog, k7) 3 times, k2tog, k5 (35 sts).
Cast off kwise.

ARMS AND HANDS

Make arms and hands in E, as for Skateboarder on pages 13 and 14.

HAIR

Make hair in I, as for Groom on page 48.

JACKET

Note: Sleeves are worked first and knitted into body.

Sleeves (make 2)

Beg at cuff using the long tail method and D, cast on 16 sts.
Row 1 (RS): Purl.
Rows 2 to 9: Beg with a p row, work 8 rows in st-st, finishing with a RS row.

Row 10: Cast off 3 sts pwise, p9, cast off rem 3 sts pwise and fasten off (10 sts).
Set aside.
Rep second sleeve as for first sleeve and set aside.

Front and back

Using the long tail method and D, cast on 38 sts.
Row 1 (RS): Purl.
Rows 2 to 6: Beg with a p row, work 5 rows in st-st and k the first 2 and last 2 sts on every p row.
Rows 7 and 8: P 1 row then k 1 row.
Row 9: Knit.
Row 10: K2, p to last 2 sts, k2.
Row 11: Knit.

Divide for armholes
Row 12: K2, p6, cast off 4 sts pwise, p13, cast off 4 sts pwise, p5, k2 (30 sts).

Join sleeves
Row 13: With RS of all pieces facing, k8 from right front, k10 from one sleeve, k14 across back, k10 from other sleeve, k8 from left front (50 sts).
Row 14: K2, p4, (p2tog) twice, p6, (p2tog) twice, p10, (p2tog) twice, p6, (p2tog) twice, p4, k2 (42 sts).
Row 15: K5, (k2tog) twice, k4, (k2tog) twice, k8, (k2tog) twice, k4, (k2tog) twice, k5, (34 sts).

Row 16: K2, p to last 2 sts, k2.
Row 17: K4, (k2tog) twice, k2, (k2tog) twice, k6, (k2tog) twice, k2, (k2tog) twice, k4 (26 sts).
Row 18: K2, p to last 2 sts, k2.

Work collar
Rows 19 and 20: Work 2 rows in g-st.
Row 21: (K2, m1) twice, k to last 4 sts, (m1, k2) twice (30 sts).
Rows 22 to 24: Work 3 rows in g-st.
Cast off in g-st.

CRAVAT
Using the long tail method and H, cast on 5 sts and work in moss-st.
Row 1 (WS): K1, (p1, k1) to end.
Rows 2 to 11: Rep row 1, 10 times more.
Cast off in moss-st.

DEER-STALKER HAT
Beg at lower edge using the long tail method and F, cast on 40 sts, RS facing to beg.
Rows 1 to 6: Beg with a k row, work 6 rows in st-st.
Row 7: (K2tog, k3) to end (32 sts).
Row 8 and foll 2 alt rows: Purl.
Row 9: (K2tog, k2) to end (24 sts).
Row 11: (K2tog, k1) to end (16 sts).
Row 13: (K2tog) to end (8 sts).
Thread yarn through sts on needle, pull tight and secure by threading yarn a second time through sts.

Front peak
Using the long tail method and F, cast on 8 sts, WS facing to beg.
Rows 1 to 7: Beg with a p row, work 7 rows in st-st.
Cast off.

Back peak
Using the long tail method and F, cast on 12 sts, WS facing to beg.
Rows 1 to 5: Beg with a p row, work 5 rows in st-st.
Cast off.

Flaps (make 2)
Using the long tail method and F, cast on 18 sts, WS facing to beg.
Rows 1 to 7: Beg with a p row, work 7 rows in st-st.
Row 8: (K2tog, k1) to end (12 sts).
Row 9: Purl.
Row 10: (K2tog) to end (6 sts).
Thread yarn through sts on needle, pull tight and secure by threading yarn a second time through sts.

STICK

Using the long tail method and J, cast on 6 sts and work in rev st-st, RS facing to beg.

Beg with a p row, work in st-st for 3¼in (8cm), finishing with a p row.

Shape top of stick

Row 1: K1, (m1, k1) to end (11 sts).
Rows 2 and 3: P 1 row then k 1 row.
Thread yarn through sts on needle, pull tight and secure by threading yarn a second time through sts.

MAKING UP

Note: Sew up all row-end seams on right side using mattress stitch one stitch in from the edge, unless otherwise stated; a one-stitch seam allowance has been allowed for this.

Shoes, legs, body and head

Make up shoes, legs, body and head, as for Skateboarder on page 15.

Breeches

Sew up leg seams of breeches and sew round crotch. Sew up row ends at centre back and place breeches on doll. Sew cast-off stitches of breeches to first row of upper body all the way round.

Arms, hands and features

Make up arms, hands and work features, as for Skateboarder on page 15.

Hair

Make up hair, as for Groom on page 51.

Jacket and cravat

Sew up sleeve seams of jacket and sew across under arm. Place jacket on doll and turn collar back. Sew cravat to front of neck and tuck inside jacket. Sew up centre front of jacket.

Deer-stalker hat

Sew up row ends of hat and place on head. Sew lower edge of hat to head. Fold peaks for back and front, bringing cast-on and cast-off stitches together, and oversew these edges. Gather round row ends, pull tight and secure. Sew peaks to front and back of hat. Sew up row ends of flaps and with this seam at centre of inside edge, sew flaps to sides of hat. To make a bow, make a twisted cord (see page 218) out of one strand of bottle green, beginning with the yarn 24in (60cm) long. Tie twisted cord into a small bow. Sew bow to top of deer-stalker hat, sewing through knot of bow to secure, then knot and trim ends to ½in (13mm).

Stick

Cut plastic drinking straw to 3½in (9cm). Place stick around straw and oversew row ends from bottom of stick to wide part at top, enclosing straw inside. Place a small ball of stuffing into top of stick using tweezers or tip of scissors and finish sewing up row ends. Sew stick to hand of doll.

Sailor

Materials

- ♥ Any DK (US: light worsted) yarn
  (amounts given are approximate):
  5g black (A)
  5g pale pink (B)
  5g white (C)
  10g royal blue (D)
  5g brown (E)
- ♥ Oddments of black, red and royal blue
  for embroidery and red for making up
- ♥ 1 pair of 3.25mm (UK10:US3) needles
  and a spare needle of the same size
- ♥ Knitters' pins and a blunt-ended needle
  for sewing up
- ♥ Tweezers (optional)
- ♥ Acrylic toy stuffing
- ♥ A red pencil for shading cheeks

Finished size

Sailor stands 6in (15cm) tall

Tension

26 sts x 34 rows measure 4in (10cm)
square over st-st using 3.25mm needles
and DK yarn before stuffing

Abbreviations

See page 219

How to make Sailor

BOOTS, LEGS, BODY AND HEAD
Right leg
Using the long tail method and A for boot, cast on 14 sts.
Place a marker on cast-on edge between the 5th and 6th st of the sts just cast on.
Row 1 (WS): Purl.
Row 2: K2, (m1, k2) to end (20 sts).
Rows 3 to 5: Beg with a p row, work 3 rows in st-st.
Row 6: K2, (k2tog) 6 times, k6 (14 sts).
Row 7: P7, p2tog, p1, p2tog, p2 (12 sts).
Rows 8 and 9: K 1 row then p 1 row.
Rows 10 to 21: Change to B for leg and beg with a k row, work 12 rows in st-st.
Break yarn and set aside.

Left leg
Using the long tail method and A for boot, cast on 14 sts.
Place a marker on cast-on edge between the 9th and 10th st of the sts just cast on.
Row 1 (WS): Purl.
Row 2: K2, (m1, k2) to end (20 sts).
Rows 3 to 5: Beg with a p row, work 3 rows in st-st.
Row 6: K6, (k2tog) 6 times, k2 (14 sts).
Row 7: P2, p2tog, p1, p2tog, p7 (12 sts).
Rows 8 and 9: K 1 row then p 1 row.
Rows 10 to 21: Change to B for leg and beg with a k row, work 12 rows in st-st.

Join legs
Row 22: Change to C for lower body and with RS facing, k across sts of left leg then with the same yarn cont k across sts of right leg (24 sts).
Rows 23 to 27: Beg with a p row, work 5 rows in st-st.
Rows 28 to 37: Change to B for upper body and work 10 rows in st-st.
Place a marker on last row for neck gathering.

Rows 38 and 39: Work 2 rows in st-st.
Row 40: K2, (m1, k4) to last 2 sts, m1, k2 (30 sts).
Rows 41 to 49: Beg with a p row, work 9 rows in st-st.
Row 50: (K2tog, k1) to end (20 sts).
Row 51: Purl.
Row 52: (K2tog) to end (10 sts).
Thread yarn through sts on needle and leave loose.

TROUSERS, ARMS, HANDS AND HAIR
Make trousers in D, arms and hands in B and hair in E, as for Skateboarder on pages 13 and 14.

TUNIC
Note: Sleeves are worked first and knitted into body.

Sleeves (make 2)
Beg at cuff using the long tail method and D, cast on 16 sts, RS facing to beg.

Rows 1 and 2: P 2 rows.
Rows 3 and 4: Join on C and work 2 rows in g-st.
Rows 5 to 11: Cont in D and beg with a k row, work 7 rows in st-st, finishing with a RS row.
Row 12: Cast off 3 sts pwise, p9, cast off rem 3 sts pwise and fasten off (10 sts).
Set aside.
Rep second sleeve as for first sleeve and set aside.

Front and back
Using the long tail method and D, cast on 38 sts, RS facing to beg.
Rows 1 and 2: P 2 rows.
Rows 3 and 4: Join on C and work 2 rows in g-st.
Rows 5 to 11: Cont in D and beg with a k row, work 7 rows in st-st, finishing with a RS row.

Divide for armholes

Row 12: P8, cast off 4 sts pwise, p13, cast off 4 sts pwise, p7 (30 sts).

Join sleeves

Row 13: With RS of all pieces facing, k8 from left back, k10 from one sleeve, k14 across front, k10 from other sleeve, k8 from right back (50 sts).

Row 14: P6, (p2tog) twice, p6, (p2tog) twice, p10, (p2tog) twice, p6, (p2tog) twice, p6 (42 sts).

Row 15: K5, (k2tog) twice, k4, (k2tog) twice, k8, (k2tog) twice, k4, (k2tog) twice, k5 (34 sts).

Row 16: Purl.

Row 17: K4, (k2tog) twice, k2, (k2tog) twice, k6, (k2tog) twice, k2, (k2tog) twice, k4 (26 sts).
Cast off kwise.

COLLAR

Using the long tail method and C, cast on 36 sts and work in g-st.

Row 1 (RS): K13, kfb, turn.

Row 2: S1k, k11, turn.

Row 3: S1k, k9, kfb, turn.

Row 4: S1k, k8, turn.

Row 5: S1k, k6, kfb, turn.

Row 6: S1k, k5, turn.

Row 7: S1k, k3, kfb, turn.

Row 8: S1k, cast off next 14 sts kwise and fasten off (26 sts).

Row 9: Rejoin yarn to rem sts and k23, turn.

Rows 10 to 14: Rep rows 3 to 7 once.

Row 15: S1k, k to end (29 sts).

Row 16: Cast off 13 sts kwise, k to end (16 sts).

Rows 17 to 21: Work 5 rows in g-st.
Cast off in g-st.

HAT

Beg at lower edge using the long tail method and C, cast on 30 sts.

Row 1 (RS): Knit.

Row 2: P1, (m1, p2) to last st, m1, p1 (45 sts).

Rows 3 and 4: K 1 row then p 1 row.

Rows 5 and 6: Join on D and work 2 rows in g-st.

Rows 7 and 8: Cont in C and work 2 rows in g-st.

Rows 9 and 10: K 1 row then p 1 row.

Row 11: (K2tog, k3) to end (36 sts).

Row 12 and foll 2 alt rows: Purl.

Row 13: (K2tog, k2) to end (27 sts).

Row 15: (K2tog, k1) to end (18 sts).

Row 17: (K2tog) to end (9 sts).
Thread yarn through sts on needle, pull tight and secure by threading yarn a second time through sts.

Ribbon

Using the long tail method and D, cast on 8 sts.
Cast off kwise.

MAKING UP

Note: Sew up all row-end seams on right side using mattress stitch one stitch in from the edge, unless otherwise stated; a one-stitch seam allowance has been allowed for this.

Boots, legs, body and head

Sew up row ends of boots. With markers at tips of toes, oversew cast-on stitches; leg seam will be ¼in (6mm) on inside edge of heel. Place a ball of stuffing into toes, sew up row ends of legs and sew round crotch. Stuff legs, sew up row ends of body and head, and stuff body and head. Pull stitches on a thread tight at top of head and fasten off. To shape neck, take a double piece of pale pink yarn and sew a running stitch round row with marker on at neck, sewing in and out of every half stitch. Pull tight, knot yarn and sew ends into neck.

Trousers, arms, hands, features and hair

Make up trousers, arms, hands, work features and make up hair, as for Skateboarder on page 15.

Tunic, collar and bow

Sew up sleeve seams of tunic and sew across under arm. Place tunic on doll and sew up back seam. Sew neck to doll all the way round. Embroider a royal blue line round collar using stem stitch one garter stitch ridge in from outside edge. Pin and sew collar around neck and join at centre front. To make bow, make a twisted cord (see page 218) out of two strands of red yarn, beginning with the yarn 36in (90cm) long. Tie twisted cord into a small bow. Sew bow to front of tunic, sewing through knot of bow to secure, and knot and trim ends to ¼in (6mm).

Hat and ribbon

Sew up row ends of hat and place on head. Sew lower edge of hat to head all the way round. Fold ribbon in half and sew fold to side of hat.

Chimney Sweep

Materials

- ♥ Any DK (US: light worsted) yarn (amounts given are approximate):
  5g black (A)
  5g pale pink (B)
  5g white (C)
  5g terracotta (D)
  5g charcoal (E)
  5g brown (F)
  5g cherry red (G)
  5g dark grey (H)
  2g yellow (I)
  2g blue (J)
- ♥ Oddments of black and red for embroidery
- ♥ 1 pair of 3.25mm (UK10:US3) needles and a spare needle of the same size
- ♥ Knitters' pins and a blunt-ended needle for sewing up
- ♥ Tweezers (optional)
- ♥ Acrylic toy stuffing
- ♥ A red pencil and a lead pencil for shading cheeks
- ♥ Wooden dowelling ¼in (6mm) in thickness, 7in (18cm) long

Finished size

Chimney Sweep stands 6in (15cm) tall

Tension

26 sts x 34 rows measure 4in (10cm) square over st-st using 3.25mm needles and DK yarn before stuffing

Abbreviations

See page 219

How to make Chimney Sweep

SHOES, LEGS, BODY, HEAD, TROUSERS, ARMS, HANDS AND HAIR

Make shoes, legs, body, head, trousers, arms, hands and hair using A for shoes, B for legs, C for lower body, D for upper body and B for head and make trousers in E, arms and hands in B and hair in F, as for Skateboarder on pages 13 and 14.

JUMPER

Note: Sleeves are worked first and knitted into body.

Sleeves (make 2)

Beg at cuff using the long tail method and D, cast on 16 sts, RS facing to beg.
Rows 1 and 2: P 1 row then k 1 row.
Rows 3 to 11: Beg with a k row, work 9 rows in st-st, finishing with a RS row.

Row 12: Cast off 3 sts pwise, p9, cast off rem 3 sts and fasten off (10 sts). Set aside.
Rep second sleeve as for first sleeve and set aside.

Front and back

Using the long tail method and D, cast on 38 sts, RS facing to beg.
Rows 1 and 2: P 1 row then k 1 row.
Rows 3 to 9: Beg with a k row, work 7 rows in st-st, finishing with a RS row.

Divide for armholes

Row 10: P8, cast off 4 sts pwise, p13, cast off 4 sts pwise, p7 (30 sts).

Join sleeves

Row 11: With RS of all pieces facing, k8 from left back, k10 from one sleeve, k14 across front, k10 from other sleeve, k8 from right back (50 sts).
Row 12: P6, (p2tog) twice, p6, (p2tog) twice, p10, (p2tog) twice, p6, (p2tog) twice, p6 (42 sts).
Row 13: K5, (k2tog) twice, k4, (k2tog) twice, k8, (k2tog) twice, k4, (k2tog) twice, k5 (34 sts).
Row 14: Purl.
Row 15: K4, (k2tog) twice, k2, (k2tog) twice, k6, (k2tog) twice, k2, (k2tog) twice, k4 (26 sts).
Row 16: Purl.
Cast off.

SCARF

Scarf tails
Using the long tail method and G, cast on 5 sts and work in g-st, RS facing to beg.
Rows 1 to 34: Work 34 rows in g-st.
Cast off in g-st.

Neck piece
Using the thumb method and G, cast on 5 sts and work in g-st, RS facing to beg.
Rows 1 to 51: Work 51 rows in g-st.
Cast off in g-st.

CAP
Make cap in H, as for Painter & Decorator on page 30.

PATCHES (Make 2: 1 in I and 1 in J)
Using the long tail method and I or J, cast on 5 sts and work in g-st, RS facing to beg.
Rows 1 to 3: Work 3 rows in g-st.
Cast off in g-st.

BRUSH
Using the long tail method and A, cast on 10 sts, WS facing to beg.
Row 1 and foll 2 alt rows: Purl.
Row 2: (Kfb) to end (20 sts).
Row 4: (Kfb, k1) to end (30 sts).
Rows 6 to 14: Work 9 rows in g-st finishing with a RS row.
Row 15 and foll alt row: Purl.
Row 16: (K2tog, k1) to end (20 sts).
Row 18: (K2tog) to end (10 sts)
Cast off pwise.

Pole
Using the long tail method and A, cast on 6 sts.
Beg with a p row, work in st-st for 7½in (19cm).
Cast off.

MAKING UP
Note: Sew up all row-end seams on right side using mattress stitch one stitch in from the edge, unless otherwise stated; a one-stitch seam allowance has been allowed for this.

Shoes, legs, body, head, trousers, arms, hands, features and hair
Make up shoes, legs, body, head, trousers, arms, hands, work features and make up hair, as for Skateboarder on page 15. Using picture as a guide, shade charcoal smudges on face with a lead pencil.

Jumper

Make up jumper, as for Union Jack Doll on page 74.

Scarf

Fold scarf tails in half and sew fold to front of neck. Place scarf around neck, sew up cast-on and cast-off stitches at back and sew all edges down.

Cap

Make up cap, as for Painter & Decorator on page 31.

Patches

Sew one patch to jumper and one patch to trousers.

Brush

Cut dowelling to 7in (18cm) and place pole around dowelling then oversew row ends along length, enclosing dowelling inside. Gather round top and bottom, pull tight and secure. Sew up row ends of brush and bring cast-on and cast-off stitches together. Place this edge on top of pole and stitch in place. Sew pole to hand of doll.

Stars & Stripes Doll

Materials

- ♥ Any DK (US: light worsted) yarn (amounts given are approximate):
  10g red (A)
  10g white (B)
  5g pale pink (C)
  5g royal blue (D)
  5g brown (E)
- ♥ Oddments of black, red and white for embroidery
- ♥ 1 pair of 3.25mm (UK10:US3) needles and a spare needle of the same size
- ♥ Knitters' pins and a blunt-ended needle for sewing up
- ♥ Tweezers (optional)
- ♥ Acrylic toy stuffing
- ♥ A red pencil for shading cheeks

Finished size

Stars & Stripes Doll stands 7³/4in (19.5cm) tall

Tension

26 sts x 34 rows measure 4in (10cm) square over st-st using 3.25mm needles and DK yarn before stuffing

Abbreviations

See page 219

How to make Stars & Stripes Doll

SHOES, LEGS, BODY AND HEAD
Right leg
Using the long tail method and A for shoe, cast on 14 sts.

Place a marker on cast-on edge between the 5th and 6th st of the sts just cast on.

Row 1 (WS): Purl.

Row 2: K2, (m1, k2) to end (20 sts).

Rows 3 to 5: Beg with a p row, work 3 rows in st-st.

Row 6: K2, (k2tog) 6 times, k6 (14 sts).

Row 7: P7, p2tog, p1, p2tog, p2 (12 sts).

Rows 8 to 21: Change to B for leg and work 14 rows in st-st.

Break yarn and set aside.

Left leg
Using the long tail method and A for shoe, cast on 14 sts.

Place a marker on cast-on edge between the 9th and 10th st of the sts just cast on.

Row 1 (WS): Purl.

Row 2: K2, (m1, k2) to end (20 sts).

Rows 3 to 5: Beg with a p row, work 3 rows in st-st.

Row 6: K6, (k2tog) 6 times, k2 (14 sts).

Row 7: P2, p2tog, p1, p2tog, p7 (12 sts).

Rows 8 to 21: Change to B for leg and work 14 rows in st-st.

Join legs
Row 22: With RS facing, k across sts of left leg then with the same yarn cont k across sts of right leg (24 sts).

Place a marker on first and last st of last row.

Rows 23 to 27: Beg with a p row, work 5 rows in st-st.

Rows 28 to 37: Change to A for upper body and work 10 rows in st-st.

Rows 38 and 39: Change to C for head and work 2 rows in st-st.

Row 40: K2, (m1, k4) to last 2 sts, m1, k2 (30 sts).

Rows 41 to 49: Beg with a p row, work 9 rows in st-st.

Row 50: (K2tog, k1) to end (20 sts).

Row 51: Purl.

Row 52: (K2tog) to end (10 sts).

Thread yarn through sts on needle and leave loose.

TROUSERS, ARMS, HANDS AND HAIR

Make trousers in B, arms and hands in C and hair in E, as for Skateboarder on pages 13 and 14.

JUMPER
Right half of jumper

Using the long tail method and D, cast on 20 sts and beg in g-st, RS facing to beg.

Rows 1 and 2: Work 2 rows in g-st.
Rows 3 and 8: Beg with a k row, work 6 rows in st-st.

Work right front

Row 9: K10, turn and work on these 10 sts.
Rows 10 to 18: Beg with a p row, work 9 rows in st-st.
Cast off 6 sts pwise, cast off rem sts kwise.

Work right back

Row 19: Rejoin yarn to sts on needle, and k to end (10 sts).
Rows 20 and 28: Beg with a p row, work 9 rows in st-st.
Cast off 2 sts kwise, cast off rem sts pwise.

Left half of jumper

Using the long tail method and A, cast on 20 sts and beg in g-st, RS facing to beg.

Rows 1 and 2: Work 2 rows in g-st.
Rows 3 and 4: Join on B and k 1 row then p 1 row.
Rows 5 to 8: Work 4 rows in st-st in stripes, 2 rows A then 2 rows B.

Work left back

Row 9: Using A, k10, turn and work on these 10 sts.
Row 10: Purl.

Rows 11 to 18: Work 8 rows in st-st in stripes, 2 rows B then 2 rows A and rep this.
Cast off 6 sts pwise and cast off rem sts kwise, using A.

Work left front

Row 19: Rejoin A to sts on needle and k to end (10 sts).
Row 20: Purl.
Rows 21 to 28: Work 8 rows in st-st in stripes, 2 rows B then 2 rows A and rep this.
Cast off 2 sts kwise and cast off rem sts pwise, using A.

Sleeves (make 2: right sleeve in A and left sleeve in D)

Beg at cuff using the long tail method and A or D, cast on 16 sts and beg in g-st, RS facing to beg.
Rows 1 and 2: Work 2 rows in g-st.
Rows 3 to 12: Beg with a k row, work 10 rows in st-st.
Cast off.

TOP HAT

Using the long tail method and B, cast on 36 sts and beg in g-st, RS facing to beg.

Rows 1 and 2: Work 2 rows in g-st. Change to D and dec:

Row 3: (K2tog, k1) to end (24 sts).

Rows 4 to 6: Beg with a p row, work 3 rows in st-st.

Rows 7 and 8: Change to A and work 2 rows in g-st.

Rows 9 to 18: Beg with a k row work 10 rows in st-st.

Rows 19 and 20: P 2 rows for fold line.

Row 21: (K2tog, k1) to end (16 sts).

Row 22: Purl.

Row 23: (K2tog) to end (8 sts). Thread yarn through sts on needle, pull tight and secure by threading yarn a second time through sts.

MAKING UP

Note: Sew up all row-end seams on right side using mattress stitch one stitch in from the edge, unless otherwise stated; a one-stitch seam allowance has been allowed for this.

Shoes, legs, body and head

Sew up row ends of shoes and with markers at tips of toes, oversew cast-on stitches; leg seam will be ¼in (6mm) on inside edge of heel. Place a ball of stuffing into toes and sew up row ends of legs. Bring markers together at crotch and sew round crotch. Stuff legs, sew up row ends of body and head, and stuff body and head. Pull stitches on a thread tight at top of head and fasten off. To shape neck, take a double piece of yarn to match body and sew a running stitch round last row of body at neck, sewing in and out of every half stitch. Pull tight, knot yarn and sew ends into neck.

Trousers, arms, hands, features and hair

Make up trousers, arms, hands, work features and make up hair, as for Skateboarder on page 15.

Jumper and embroidery

Sew up shoulder of seams of jumper and sew up row ends of sleeves. Sew sleeves into armholes. Embroider stars in white on right half of jumper. Place halves of jumper together and sew fronts together. Place jumper on doll and sew up back seam.

Top hat

Make up top hat, as for Union Jack Doll on page 75.

Graduate

Materials

- ♥ Any DK (US: light worsted) yarn (amounts given are approximate):
  15g black (A)
  5g pale pink (B)
  5g white (C)
  5g silver grey (D)
  5g claret (E)
  5g brown (F)
  5g red (G)
  5g green (H)
- ♥ Oddments of black and red for embroidery and black and red for making up
- ♥ 1 pair of 3.25mm (UK10:US3) needles and a spare needle of the same size
- ♥ Knitters' pins and a blunt-ended needle for sewing up
- ♥ Tweezers (optional)
- ♥ Acrylic toy stuffing
- ♥ A red pencil for shading cheeks
- ♥ Small piece of thick cardboard

Finished size

Graduate stands 6½in (16.5cm) tall

Tension

26 sts x 34 rows measure 4in (10cm) square over st-st using 3.25mm needles and DK yarn before stuffing

Abbreviations

See page 219

How to make Graduate

Note: Follow individual instructions for boy doll or girl doll.

SHOES, LEGS, BODY AND HEAD FOR BOY DOLL

Make shoes, legs, body and head using A for shoes, B for legs, A for lower body, C for upper body and B for head, as for Skateboarder on page 13.

SLIPPERS, LEGS, BODY AND HEAD FOR GIRL DOLL

Make slippers, legs, body and head using A for slippers, B for legs, A for lower body, C for upper body and B for head, as for Valentine on page 21.

TROUSERS FOR BOY DOLL

Make trousers in D, as for Skateboarder on page 13.

SKIRT FOR GIRL DOLL

Using the long tail method and E, cast on 40 sts.
Row 1 (RS): Purl.
Rows 2 to 16: Beg with a p row, work 15 rows in st-st.
Row 17: (K2tog, k2) to end (30 sts).
Cast off pwise.

SLEEVES AND HANDS
(make 2)

Make sleeves and hands using C for sleeve and B for hand, as for Doctor on page 61.

HAIR FOR BOY DOLL

Make hair in F, as for Skateboarder on page 14.

HAIR FOR GIRL DOLL

Make hair in F, as for Valentine on page 22.

COLLAR

Beg at lower edge using the long tail method and C, cast on 26 sts and work in g-st, RS facing to beg.
Row 1: K5, turn.
Row 2: S1k, k to end.
Row 3: Knit.
Rows 4 and 5: Rep rows 1 and 2 once.
Cast off in g-st.

GOWN

Note: Sleeves are worked first and knitted into body.

Sleeves (make 2)

Beg at cuff using the long tail method and A, cast on 16 sts and beg in g-st, RS facing to beg.
Rows 1 and 2: Work 2 rows in g-st.
Rows 3 to 9: Beg with a k row, work 7 rows in st-st, finishing with a RS row.
Row 10: Cast off 3 sts pwise, p9, cast off rem 3 sts pwise and fasten off (10 sts).
Set aside.
Rep second sleeve as for first sleeve and set aside.

Front and back

Using the long tail method and A, cast on 46 sts and beg in g-st, RS facing to beg.

Rows 1 and 2: Work 2 rows in g-st.
Row 3: Knit.
Row 4: K2, p to last 2 sts, k2.
Rows 5 to 10: Rep rows 3 and 4, 3 times more.
Row 11: *K8, k2tog, k3, k2tog, k8; rep from * once (42 sts).
Rows 12 to 16: Rep row 4 once, then rep rows 3 and 4 twice more.
Row 17: *K7, k2tog, k3, k2tog, k7; rep from * once (38 sts).

Divide for armholes

Row 18: K2, p6, cast off 4 sts pwise, p13, cast off 4 sts pwise, p5, k2 (30 sts).

Join sleeves

Row 19: With RS of all pieces facing, k8 from right front, k10 from one sleeve, k14 across back, k10 from other sleeve, k8 from left front (50 sts).

Row 20: K2, p4, (p2tog) twice, p6, (p2tog) twice, p10, (p2tog) twice, p6, (p2tog) twice, p4, k2 (42 sts).
Row 21: *K2, (k2tog, k3) 3 times, k2tog, k2; rep from * to end once (34 sts).
Cast off kwise.

HOOD

Using the long tail method and G, cast on 60 sts.
Row 1 (RS): K2tog, k to last 2 sts, k2tog (58 sts).
Row 2: P2tog, p to last 2 sts, p2tog (56 sts).
Change to H and dec:
Row 3: K2tog, k18, (k2tog, k2) twice, (k2, k2tog) twice, k18, k2tog (50 sts).
Row 4: Cast off 12 sts kwise, k25, cast off rem 12 sts and fasten off (26 sts).
Join A to rem sts and dec:
Row 5: K5, (k2tog, k2) twice, (k2, k2tog) twice, k5 (22 sts).
Row 6 and foll alt row: Purl.
Row 7: K5, (k2tog, k1) twice, (k1, k2tog) twice, k5 (18 sts).

Row 9: K5, (k2tog) 4 times, k5 (14 sts).
Cast off pwise.

MORTARBOARD
Cap

Using the long tail method and A, cast on 14 sts and work in g-st, RS facing to beg.
Rows 1 to 25: Work 25 rows in g-st.
Cast off in g-st.

Top piece

Using the long tail method and A, cast on 20 sts, WS facing to beg.
Rows 1 to 27: Beg with a p row, work 27 rows in st-st.
Cast off.

DIPLOMA

Using the long tail method and C, cast on 12 sts, RS facing to beg.
Rows 1 to 12: Beg with a k row, work 15 rows in st-st and k the first and last st on every p row.
Cast off kwise.

MAKING UP

Note: Sew up all row-end seams on right side using mattress stitch one stitch in from the edge, unless otherwise stated; a one-stitch seam allowance has been allowed for this.

Shoes, legs, body and head for Boy Doll

Make up shoes, legs, body and head, as for Skateboarder on page 15.

Slippers, legs, body and head for Girl Doll

Make up slippers, legs, body and head, as for Valentine on page 23.

Trousers or skirt

Make up trousers, as for Skateboarder on page 15. Sew up row ends of skirt and place on doll. Sew cast-off stitches of skirt to first row of upper body, all the way round.

Sleeves and hands

Make up sleeves and hands, as for Doctor on page 63.

Features

Work features, as for Skateboarder on page 15.

Hair

Make up hair for Boy Doll, as for Skateboarder on page 15. Make up hair for Girl Doll, as for Valentine on page 23.

Collar

Place collar around neck and sew together beneath chin. Sew all edges of collar down.

Gown

Sew up sleeve seams of gown and sew across under arm. Place gown on doll and overlap front bands and sew together down centre front. Sew around yoke.

Hood

Fold cast-off stitches of centre of hood in half and oversew. Place hood around neck and oversew shaped row ends at front. Pin and sew cast-off stitches to neck of gown and across back.

Mortarboard

Place cap on head and pin and sew all edges down. Cut a piece of thick cardboard 2in (5cm) square and place on wrong side of top piece. Bring two corners of the knitting together and sew together, then bring the remaining two corners together and sew all edges together. Place top piece on head and sew the centre to top of cap. To make the tassel, cut eight lengths of black yarn 8in (20cm) long and lay them in a bundle. Tie bundle in middle and fold tassel in half. Wind black yarn tightly around tassel below knot and secure. Sew tassel to top of mortarboard and trim ends.

Diploma

With right side outside, roll diploma up and sew in place. Make a twisted cord (see page 218) out of one strand of red, beginning with the yarn 32in (80cm) long. Tie twisted cord round diploma making a bow and sew through knot to secure. Knot and trim ends of bow to ½in (13mm). Sew diploma to hand of doll.

Scarecrow

Materials

- ♥ Any DK (US: light worsted) yarn (amounts given are approximate):
  10g beige (A)
  5g dull green (B)
  10g brown (C)
  5g grey (D)
  2g deep red (E)
- ♥ Oddments of black and dark brown for embroidery and rust and 5g of lemon for making up
- ♥ 1 pair of 3.25mm (UK10:US3) needles and a spare needle of the same size
- ♥ Knitters' pins and a blunt-ended needle for sewing up
- ♥ Tweezers (optional)
- ♥ Acrylic toy stuffing

Finished size

Scarecrow stands 6½in (16.5cm) tall

Tension

26 sts x 34 rows measure 4in (10cm) square over st-st using 3.25mm needles and DK yarn before stuffing

Abbreviations

See page 219

How to make Scarecrow

LEGS, BODY AND HEAD
Right leg
Beg at ankle using the long tail method and A, cast on 12 sts, WS facing to beg.
Rows 1 to 13: Beg with a p row, work 13 rows in st-st.
Break yarn and set aside.

Left leg
Work left leg as for right leg but do not break yarn.

Join legs
Row 14: With RS facing, k across sts of left leg then with the same yarn cont k across sts of right leg (24 sts). Place a marker on first and last st of last row.
Rows 15 to 29: Beg with a p row, work 15 rows in st-st.
Place markers for arms on the 7th and 18th sts of last row.
Rows 30 to 41: Work 12 rows in st-st.
Row 42: (K2tog, k1) to end (16 sts).
Row 43: Purl.
Row 44: (K2tog) to end (8 sts).
Thread yarn through sts on needle and leave loose.

TROUSERS
Make trousers in B, as for Skateboarder on page 13.

ARMS (make 2)
Beg at shoulder using the long tail method and A, cast on 11 sts, WS facing to beg.
Rows 1 to 7: Beg with a p row, work 7 rows in st-st.
Cast off.

COAT
Using the long tail method and C, cast on 44 sts and beg in g-st, RS facing to beg.
Rows 1 and 2: Work 2 rows in g-st.
Row 3: Knit.
Row 4: K2, p to last 2 sts, k2.
Rows 5 to 10: Rep rows 3 and 4, 3 times more.
Row 11: (K6, k2tog) twice, k12, (k2tog, k6) twice (40 sts).
Rows 12 to 16: Rep row 4 once, then rep rows 3 and 4 twice more.
Row 17: (K6, k2tog) twice, k8, (k2tog, k6) twice (36 sts).

Divide for armholes
Row 18: K2, p7, cast off 2 sts pwise, p13, cast off 2 sts pwise, p6, k2 (32 sts).

Work right front
Row 19: K9, turn and work on these 9 sts.
Row 20: P7, k2.
Row 21: Knit.
Row 22: P6, k3.
Row 23: Knit.
Row 24: P5, k4.
Row 25: Knit.
Row 26: P4, k5.

Rows 27 to 31: Rep rows 25 and 26, twice more then row 25 once.
Row 32: Cast off 3 sts pwise, k5 (6 sts).
Row 33: K4, k2tog (5 sts).
Rows 34 to 42: Work 9 rows in g-st. Cast off in g-st.

Work back
Row 43: Rejoin yarn to rem sts and k14, turn and work on these 14 sts.
Rows 44 to 52: Beg with a p row, work 9 rows in st-st.

Rows 53 and 54: Cast off 3 sts at beg of next 2 rows (8 sts).
Cast off.

Work left front
Row 55: Rejoin yarn to rem sts and k9 (9 sts).
Row 56: K2, p7.
Row 57: Knit.
Row 58: K3, p6.
Row 59: Knit.
Row 60: K4, p5.
Row 61: Knit.
Row 62: K5, p4.

Rows 63 to 66: Rep rows 61 and 62 twice more.
Row 67: Cast off 3 sts kwise, k5 (6 sts).
Row 68: K4, k2tog (5 sts).
Rows 69 to 78: work 10 rows in g-st. Cast off in g-st.

Sleeves (make 2)
Beg at shoulder using the long tail method and C, cast on 16 sts, WS facing to beg.
Rows 1 to 5: Beg with a p row, work 5 rows in st-st.
Rows 6 to 8: Work 3 rows in g-st. Cast off in g-st.

PATCH
Using the long tail method and D, cast on 5 sts and work in g-st, RS facing to beg.
Rows 1 to 5: Work 5 rows in g-st. Cast off in g-st.

HAT
Using the long tail method and D, cast on 40 sts and beg in g-st, RS facing to beg.
Rows 1 to 4: Work 4 rows in g-st. Change to E for hat band and dec:
Row 5: (K2tog, k2tog, k1) to end (24 sts).
Row 6: Purl.
Rows 7 to 12: Cont in D and beg with a k row, work 6 rows in st-st.
Row 13: (K2tog, k1) to end (16 sts).
Row 14: Purl.
Row 15: (K2tog) to end (8 sts).
Thread yarn through sts on needle, pull tight and secure by threading yarn a second time through sts.

MAKING UP
Note: Sew up all row-end seams on right side using mattress stitch one stitch in from the edge, unless otherwise stated; a one-stitch seam allowance has been allowed for this.

Feet, legs, body and head

Make straw feet by winding lemon
yarn 40 times round two fingers
and cut through loops. Lay flat and
tie a tight thread at middle and fold
in half. Repeat for second foot and
sew folded ends to insides of ankles.
Sew up row ends of legs around
straw feet and work back stitch
around ankles stitching into straw
feet and pull tight. Trim straw feet
to ⅔in (18mm). Sew up row ends of
legs, sew round crotch, and stuff
legs. Sew up row ends of body and
head and stuff body and head. Pull
stitches on a thread tight at top of
head and fasten off.

Trousers

Sew up leg seams of trousers and
sew round crotch. Sew up row ends
at centre back and place trousers on
doll. Sew cast-off stitches of trousers
to body all the way round.

Hands and arms

Make straw hands by winding lemon
yarn 30 times round two fingers and
cut through loops. Lay flat and tie
a tight thread at middle and fold in
half. Repeat for second hand and
sew folded ends to insides of wrists.
Sew up row ends of arms around
straw hands and work back stitch
around wrists, stitching into straw
hands, and pull tight. Sew up row
ends of arms and stuff arms. Leaving
armholes open, sew arms to body,
matching top of arms to markers.
Trim straw hands to ⅔in (18mm).

Coat

Sew up shoulder seams of coat, sew
up cast-off stitches of collar and
sew collar of coat around back of
neck. Sew up row ends of arms
and sew arms to armholes of coat,
stitching on inside edge. Place coat
on scarecrow and fold collar down.
Sew coat together at centre front.

Features, belt and patch

Mark position of eyes with two pins
on 6th row above arms, spacing two
knitted stitches apart. Embroider
eyes in black (see page 218 for how to
begin and fasten off the embroidery
invisibly), making a small chain
stitch beginning at marked position
and ending on row above, and work
a second chain stitch on top of first.
Embroider mouth in dark brown
using straight stitches on 2nd and
3rd row below eyes. Make a belt
using one strand of rust beginning
with the yarn 45in (115cm) long and
make a twisted cord (see page 218).
Tie twisted cord around waist with a
double knot and knot and trim ends.
Sew patch to coat and embroider
stitches in black.

Hat

Sew up row ends of hat and stuff top
of hat. Pin hat to top of head to one
side and sew hat to head using back
stitch, sewing through hat to head at
base of brim.

King & Queen

Materials

- ♥ Any DK (US: light worsted) yarn
  (amounts given are approximate):
  25g red (A)
  10g pale pink (B)
  10g white (C)
  5g ginger (D)
  10g gold (E)
  5g brown (F)
  10g purple (G)
- ♥ Oddments of black and red for embroidery
- ♥ 1 pair of 3.25mm (UK10:US3) needles and
  a spare needle of the same size
- ♥ Knitters' pins and a blunt-ended needle
  for sewing up
- ♥ Tweezers (optional)
- ♥ Acrylic toy stuffing
- ♥ A red pencil for shading cheeks

Finished size

King stands 6³/₄in (17cm) tall
Queen stands 6¹/₂in (16.5cm) tall

Tension

26 sts x 34 rows measure 4in (10cm)
square over st-st using 3.25mm needles
and DK yarn before stuffing

Abbreviations

See page 219

How to make King

SHOES, LEGS, BODY AND HEAD
Right leg
Using the long tail method and A for shoes, cast on 14 sts.

Place a marker on cast-on edge between the 5th and 6th st of the sts just cast on.

Row 1 (WS): Purl.

Row 2: K2, (m1, k2) to end (20 sts).

Rows 3 to 5: Beg with a p row, work 3 rows in st-st.

Row 6: K2, (k2tog) 6 times, k6 (14 sts).

Row 7: P7, p2tog, p1, p2tog, p2 (12 sts).

Rows 8 to 21: Change to B for leg and work 14 rows in st-st.

Break yarn and set aside.

Left leg
Using the long tail method and A for shoes, cast on 14 sts.

Place a marker on cast-on edge between the 9th and 10th st of the sts just cast on.

Row 1 (WS): Purl.

Row 2: K2, (m1, k2) to end (20 sts).

Rows 3 to 5: Beg with a p row, work 3 rows in st-st.

Row 6: K6, (k2tog) 6 times, k2 (14 sts).

Row 7: P2, p2tog, p1, p2tog, p7 (12 sts).

Rows 8 to 21: Change to B for leg and work 14 rows in st-st.

Join legs
Row 22: Change to C for lower body and with RS facing, cast on 3 sts at beg of left leg, k across sts of left leg, cast on 4 sts then with the same yarn cont k across sts of right leg then cast on 3 sts (34 sts).

Rows 23 to 33: Beg with a p row, work 11 rows in st-st.

Row 34: K7, (k2tog) twice, k12, (k2tog) twice, k7 (30 sts).

Row 35: Purl.

Row 36: K5, (k2tog) 3 times, k8, (k2tog) 3 times, k5 (24 sts).

Row 37: Purl.

Rows 38 and 39: Change to B for head and work 2 rows in st-st.

Row 40: K2, (m1, k4) to last 2 sts, m1, k2 (30 sts).

Rows 41 to 49: Beg with a p row, work 9 rows in st-st.

Row 50: (K2tog, k1) to end (20 sts).

Row 51: Purl.

Row 52: (K2tog) to end (10 sts).

Thread yarn through sts on needle and leave loose.

ARMS AND HANDS
(make 2)
Beg at shoulder using the long tail method and B, cast on 4 sts.

Row 1 (WS): Purl.

Row 2: K1, (m1, k1) to end (7 sts).

Row 3: Purl.

Row 4: K1, m1, k to last st, m1, k1 (9 sts).

Rows 5 and 6: Rep rows 3 and 4 once (11 sts).

Rows 7 to 15: Beg with a p row, work 9 rows in st-st.

Row 16: K2tog, (k1, k2tog) to end (7 sts).

Thread yarn through sts on needle, pull tight and secure by threading yarn a second time through sts.

ROBE

Note: Sleeves are worked first and knitted into body.

Sleeves (make 2)

Beg at cuff using the long tail method and C, cast on 16 sts and beg in g-st, RS facing to beg.

Rows 1 to 4: Work 4 rows in g-st.
Rows 5 to 7: Change to A and beg with a k row, work 3 rows in st-st, finishing with a RS row.
Row 8: Cast off 3 sts pwise, p9, cast off 3 sts pwise and fasten off (10 sts). Break yarn and set aside.
Rep second sleeve as for first sleeve and set aside.

Front and back

Note: 2 separate balls of A are needed.
Using the long tail method and C, cast on 54 sts and beg in g-st, RS facing to beg.

Rows 1 to 10: Work 10 rows in g-st. Join on 2 balls of A and rejoin C and work in intarsia, twisting yarn on WS when changing colours to avoid a hole.
Row 11: A-k24, C-k6, A-k24 (second ball).
Row 12: A-p24, C-k6, A-p24.
Rows 13 to 20: Rep rows 11 and 12, 4 times more.
Row 21: A-k11, k2tog, k2, k2tog, k7, C-k6, A-k7, k2tog, k2, k2tog, k11 (50 sts).
Row 22: A-p22, C-k6, A-p22.
Row 23: A-k22, C-k6, A-k22.
Rows 24 to 28: Rep rows 22 and 23 twice more then row 22 once.
Row 29: A-k10, k2tog, k2, k2tog, k6, C-k6, A-k6, k2tog, k2, k2tog, k10 (46 sts).

Divide for armholes

Row 30: A-p10, cast off 4 sts pwise, p5, C-k6, A-p6, cast off 4 sts pwise, p9 (38 sts).

Join sleeves

Row 31: Using A and with RS of all pieces facing, k10 from left back, k10 from one sleeve, k6, C-k6, A-k6 across front, k10 from other sleeve, k10 from right back (58 sts).
Row 32: A-p26, C-k6, A-p26.
Rows 33 and 34: Break off all colours and rejoin in C and work 2 rows in g-st.
Row 35: K1, (k4, k2tog, k2, k2tog, k4) 4 times, k1 (50 sts).
Row 36 and foll 2 alt rows: Knit.
Row 37: K1, (k3, k2tog, k2, k2tog, k3) 4 times, k1 (42 sts).
Row 39: K1, (k2, k2tog, k2, k2tog, k2) 4 times, k1 (34 sts).
Row 41: K2, (k2tog, k2) to end (26 sts). Cast off in g-st.

HAIR

Make hair in D, as for Groom on page 48.

BEARD (make 2 pieces)

Using the long tail method and D, cast on 8 sts and work in g-st.
Row 1 (RS): Knit.
Row 2: K1, m1, k to last st, m1, k1 (10 sts).
Rows 3 to 10: Rep rows 1 and 2, 4 times more (18 sts).
Row 11: K2, (k2tog, k2) to end (14 sts). Cast off in g-st.

CROWN (make 2 pieces)

Using the long tail method and E, cast on 30 sts, WS facing to beg.
Rows 1 to 5: Beg with a p row, work 5 rows in st-st.
Row 6: K6, turn and work in these 6 sts.
Row 7: P2tog tbl, p2, p2tog (4 sts).
Row 8: Knit.
Row 9: P2tog tbl, p2tog (2 sts).

Thread yarn through sts on needle, pull tight and secure by threading yarn a second time through sts.

Row 10: Rejoin yarn to rem sts and k6, turn and work on these 6 sts.

Rows 11 to 25: Rep rows 7 to 10, 3 times more, then rows 7 to 9 once. Thread yarn through sts on needle, pull tight and secure by threading yarn a second time through sts.

MAKING UP

Note: Sew up all row-end seams on right side using mattress stitch one stitch in from the edge, unless otherwise stated; a one-stitch seam allowance has been allowed for this.

Shoes, legs, body and head

Sew up row ends of shoes. With markers at tips of toes, oversew cast-on stitches; leg seam will be ¼in (6mm) on inside edge of heel. Place a ball of stuffing into toes. Sew up row ends of legs and sew across cast-off stitches at crotch. Stuff legs, sew up row ends of body and head, and stuff body and head, pushing stuffing into shoulders. Pull stitches on a thread tight at top of head and fasten off. To shape neck, take a double piece of yarn to match body and sew a running stitch round last row of body at neck, sewing in and out of every half stitch. Pull tight, knot yarn and sew ends into neck.

Arms and hands

Make up arms and hands, as for Skateboarder on page 15.

Robe

Weave in loose ends around intarsia. Sew up sleeve seams of robe and sew across under arm. Place robe on doll and sew up back seam.

Features and hair

Work features, as for Skateboarder on page 15. Make up hair, as for Groom on page 51.

Beard

Place wrong sides of two pieces of beard together, matching all edges, and oversew around outside edge. Sew beard to King, sewing sides of beard to hair.

Crown

Place wrong sides of two pieces of crown together, matching all edges, and oversew top edge around points. Sew up row ends to form a ring and oversew lower edge. Place crown on King and sew lower edge to head all the way round.

How to make Queen

SHOES, LEGS, BODY AND HEAD
Make shoes, legs, body and head using A for shoes, B for legs, C for lower body, A for upper body and B for head, as for Nurse on page 65.

SKIRT
Beg at lower edge using the long tail method and C, cast on 40 sts, WS facing to beg.
Rows 1 and 2: P 1 row then k 1 row (this part is turned under).
Row 3 (picot edge): P1, k1, (yrn, k2tog) to end.
Rows 4 and 5: K 1 row then p 1 row.

Rows 6 and 7: Join on E and work 2 rows in g-st.
Rows 8 to 25: Change to A and beg with a k row, work 18 rows in st-st.
Row 26: (K2tog, k2) to end (30 sts). Cast off pwise.

SLEEVES, HANDS AND CUFFS
Make sleeves and hands using A for sleeve, B for hand and A for cuffs, as for Cowboy on page 18.

ROBE
Beg at lower edge using the long tail method and E, cast on 34 sts and work in g-st, RS facing to beg.

Rows 1 and 2: Work 2 rows in g-st.
Rows 3 to 23: Change to G and work 21 rows in g-st, ending with a RS row.

Divide for armholes
Row 24: K6, cast off 3 sts, k15, cast off 3 sts, k5 (28 sts).
Row 25: K4, k2tog tbl, turn and work on these 5 sts.
Rows 26 to 32: Work 7 rows in g-st.
Row 33: K3, cast off 2 sts and fasten off (3 sts).
Row 34: Rejoin yarn to rem sts and k2tog, k12, k2tog tbl, turn and work on these 14 sts.

Rows 35 to 41: Work 7 rows in g-st.
Row 42: Cast off 2 sts, k9, cast off 2 sts and fasten off (10 sts).
Row 43: Rejoin yarn to rem sts and k2tog, k4, turn and work on these 5 sts.
Rows 44 to 50: Work 7 rows in g-st.
Row 51: Cast off 2 sts, k2 (3 sts).
Row 52: Push rem sts together and k 1 row (16 sts).
Rows 53 to 55: Change to E and work 3 rows in g-st.
Cast off in g-st.

Front edges
Using E and with RS facing, pick up and knit 20 sts from each front edge and work in g-st.
Rows 1 and 2: Work 2 rows in g-st.
Cast off in g-st.

HAIR
Make hair in F, as for Valentine on page 22.

CROWN
Make crown in E, as for King.

MAKING UP
Note: Sew up all row-end seams on right side using mattress stitch one stitch in from the edge, unless otherwise stated; a one-stitch seam allowance has been allowed for this.

Shoes, legs, body and head
Make up shoes, legs, body and head, as for Skateboarder on page 15.

Skirt
Sew up row ends of skirt and place on doll. Sew cast-off edge of skirt to first row of upper body all the way round.

Sleeves, hands and cuffs
Make up sleeves, hands and cuffs, as for Cowboy on page 19.

Robe
Oversew shoulder seams. Place robe on doll and sew neck of robe to neck of doll.

Features and hair
Embroider features, as for Skateboarder on page 15. Make up hair, as for Valentine on page 23.

Crown
Make up crown, as for King.

Artist

Materials

- ♥ Any DK (US: light worsted) yarn (amounts given are approximate):
  5g grey (A)
  5g pale pink (B)
  5g white (C)
  10g cream (D)
  5g duck-egg blue (E)
  5g ginger (F)
  5g navy blue (G)
  5g deep red (H)
  5g beige (I)
  2g dark grey (J)
  2g golden cream (K)
- ♥ Oddments of black, red, blue, yellow, green, silver grey for embroidery and navy blue, deep red and dark brown for making up
- ♥ 1 pair of 3.25mm (UK10:US3) needles and a spare needle of the same size
- ♥ Knitters' pins and a blunt-ended needle for sewing up
- ♥ Tweezers (optional)
- ♥ Acrylic toy stuffing
- ♥ 1 chenille stem
- ♥ A red pencil for shading cheeks

Finished size

Artist stands 6in (15cm) tall

Tension

26 sts x 34 rows measure 4in (10cm) square over st-st using 3.25mm needles and DK yarn before stuffing

Abbreviations

See page 219

How to make Artist

SHOES, LEGS, BODY, HEAD, TROUSERS, ARMS, HANDS AND HAIR

Make shoes, legs, body, head, trousers, arms, hands and hair using A for shoes, B for legs, C for lower body, D for upper body, B for head, make trousers in E, arms and hands in B and hair in F, as for Skateboarder on pages 13 and 14.

SMOCK
Front and back

Using the long tail method and D, cast on 44 sts and beg in g-st, RS facing to beg.
Rows 1 and 2: Work 2 rows in g-st.
Row 3: Knit.
Row 4: K2, p to last 2 sts, k2.

Rows 5 to 8: Rep rows 3 and 4 twice more.
Row 9: K9, k2tog, k2, k2tog, k14, k2tog, k2, k2tog, k9 (40 sts).
Row 10: As row 4.

Work right front
Row 11: K10, turn and work on these 10 sts.
Row 12: P to last 2 sts, k2.
Row 13: Knit.
Row 14: As row 12.
Row 15: K2, (p1, k1) 4 times.
Row 16: (K1, p1) 4 times, k2.
Rows 17 to 20: Rep rows 15 and 16 twice more.
Row 21: K2, (p1, k1) twice, p1, cast off rem 3 sts in moss st and fasten off.

Work back
Rejoin yarn to rem sts and dec:
Row 22: K2tog, k16, k2tog, turn and work on these 18 sts.
Rows 23 to 25: Beg with a p row, work 3 rows in st-st.
Row 26: (K1, p1) to end.
Row 27: (P1, k1) to end.
Rows 28 to 31: Rep rows 26 and 27 twice more.
Row 32: Cast off 3 sts in moss-st, moss-st 11, cast off rem 3 sts and fasten off.

Work left front

Row 33: Rejoin yarn to rem sts and k to end (10 sts).
Row 34: K2, p to end.
Row 35: Knit.
Row 36: As row 34.
Row 37: (K1, p1) 4 times, k2.
Row 38: K2, (p1, k1) 4 times.
Rows 39 to 42: Rep rows 37 and 38 twice more.
Row 43: Cast off 3 sts in moss-st, moss-st to end.

Work collar

Row 44: Push rem sts together and k 1 row (26 sts).
Row 45: (K2, m1) twice, k18, (m1, k2) twice (30 sts).
Rows 46 to 50: Work 5 rows in g-st.
Cast off in g-st.

Sleeves (make 2)

Using the long tail method and D, cast on 16 sts, RS facing to beg.
Rows 1 and 2: Work 2 rows in g-st.
Rows 3 to 10: Beg with a k row, work 8 rows in st-st.
Cast off.

BERET

Beg at lower edge using the long tail method and G, cast on 36 sts.
Row 1 (RS): Knit.
Row 2: P2, (m1, p4) to last 2 sts, m1, p2 (45 sts).
Row 3: Knit.
Row 4: P15, turn.
Row 5: S1k, k6, turn.
Row 6: S1p, p to end.
Row 7: Knit.
Rows 8 to 11: Rep rows 4 to 7 once.
Row 12: Purl.
Row 13: (K2tog, k3) to end (36 sts).
Row 14 and foll 2 alt rows: Purl.
Row 15: (K2tog, k2) to end (27 sts).
Row 17: (K2tog, k1) to end (18 sts).
Row 19: (K2tog) to end (9 sts).
Thread yarn through sts on needle and leave loose.

NECK BOW

Using the long tail method and H, cast on 30 sts.
Cast off kwise.

ARTIST'S PALETTE
(make 2 pieces)

Using the long tail method and I, cast on 26 sts, RS facing for top piece of palette and WS facing of back piece of palette to beg.
Row 1: Purl.
Row 2: K4, turn.
Row 3: S1p, p to end.
Row 4: (K2tog, k1) 3 times, k2, (k2tog, k1) 3 times, k4, k2tog (19 sts).
Row 5: Purl.
Row 6: (K2tog, k1) to end (13 sts).
Cast off pwise.

BRUSH

Using the long tail method and J, cast on 5 sts, WS facing to beg.
Rows 1 to 15: Beg with a p row, work 15 rows in st-st.
Rows 16 to 19: Change to A for bristles and work 4 rows in st-st.
Thread yarn through sts on needle, pull tight and secure by threading yarn a second time through sts.

MAKING UP

Note: Sew up all row-end seams on right side using mattress stitch one stitch in from the edge, unless otherwise stated; a one-stitch seam allowance has been allowed for this.

Shoes, legs, body, head, trousers, arms, hands, features and hair

Make up shoes, legs, body, head, trousers, arms, hands, work features and make up hair, as for Skateboarder on page 15.

Smock

Sew up shoulder seams of smock and sew up row ends of sleeves. Sew sleeves into armholes on wrong side and place smock on doll. Turn collar down and sew up centre front of smock. Embroider buttons in silver grey on front border, making two short stitches close together for each button.

Beret

Make a twisted cord (see page 218) out of two strands of yarn to match beret, beginning with the yarn 16in (40cm) long. Tie a knot ⅓in (8mm) from folded end and trim ends. Place knot into stitches on a thread at top of beret and pull stitches on a thread tight. Sew through knot on wrong side to secure. Sew up row ends of beret and place on head. Sew lower edge of beret to head all the way round. Pull beret to one side.

Neck bow

Loop neck bow into bow shape and tie with matching yarn at middle. Sew bow to neck of doll.

Artist's palette

Oversew row ends of cast-off stitches of each piece of palette and embroider paint on top piece of palette in blue, yellow, red and green, making four straight stitches close together. Place two pieces on top of each other, matching all edges. Oversew around outside edge and oversew cast-off stitches around centre. Sew artist's palette to left hand of doll.

Brush

Cut chenille stem to length of brush. Place brush around chenille stem and sew up row ends of brush, enclosing chenille stem inside. Gather round cast-on stitches, pull tight and secure. Using picture as a guide, wind dark brown yarn around neck of brush and secure. Sew brush to right hand of Artist.

Aviator

Materials

- ♥ Any DK (US: light worsted) yarn (amounts given are approximate):
  5g black (A)
  5g pale pink (B)
  5g white (C)
  5g ginger (D)
  5g light brown (E)
  5g medium brown (F)
  5g golden cream (G)
  5g red (H)
  5g dark brown (I)
- ♥ Oddments of black, red and dark brown for embroidery
- ♥ 1 pair of 3.25mm (UK10:US3) needles and a spare needle of the same size
- ♥ Knitters' pins and a blunt-ended needle for sewing up
- ♥ Tweezers (optional)
- ♥ Acrylic toy stuffing
- ♥ A red pencil for shading cheeks

Finished size

Aviator stands 6in (15cm) tall

Tension

26 sts x 34 rows measure 4in (10cm) square over st-st using 3.25mm needles and DK yarn before stuffing

Abbreviations

See page 219

How to make Aviator

SHOES, LEGS, BODY, HEAD, TROUSERS, ARMS, HANDS AND HAIR

Make shoes, legs, body, head, trousers, arms, hands and hair using A for shoes, B for legs, C for lower body, D for upper body, B for head, trousers in E, arms and hands in B and hair in F, as for Skateboarder on pages 13 and 14.

JACKET

Note: Sleeves are worked first and knitted into body.

Sleeves (make 2)

Beg at cuff using the long tail method and G, cast on 16 sts and beg in g-st, RS facing to beg.

Rows 1 and 2: Work 2 rows in g-st.
Rows 3 to 11: Change to D and beg with a k row, work 9 rows in st-st, finishing with a RS row.
Row 12: Cast off 3 sts pwise, p9, cast off rem 3 sts and fasten off (10 sts). Set aside.
Rep second sleeve as for first sleeve and set aside.

Front and back

Using the long tail method and G, cast on 38 sts and beg in g-st, RS facing to beg.

Rows 1 and 2: Work 2 rows in g-st.
Rows 3 to 9: Change to D and beg with a k row, work 7 rows in st-st, finishing with a RS row.

Divide for armholes

Row 10: P8, cast off 4 sts pwise, p13, cast off 4 sts pwise, p7 (30 sts).

Join sleeves

Row 11: With RS of all pieces facing, k8 from left back, k10 from one sleeve, k14 across front, k10 from other sleeve, k8 from right back (50 sts).
Row 12: P6, (p2tog) twice, p6, (p2tog) twice, p10, (p2tog) twice, p6, (p2tog) twice, p6 (42 sts).
Row 13: K5, (k2tog) twice, k4, (k2tog) twice, k8, (k2tog) twice, k4, (k2tog) twice, k5 (34 sts).
Row 14: Purl.
Row 15: K4, (k2tog) twice, k2, (k2tog) twice, k6, (k2tog) twice, k2, (k2tog) twice, k4 (26 sts).
Row 16: Purl.
Cast off.

Trim at front

Using the long tail method and G, cast on 12 sts.
Row 1 (RS): Knit.
Cast off kwise.

SCARF
Scarf tails

Using the long tail method and H, cast on 3 sts and work in g-st, RS facing to beg.
Rows 1 to 24: Work 24 rows in g-st.
Cast off in g-st.

Neck piece

Using the long tail method and H, cast on 3 sts and work in g-st, RS facing to beg.
Rows 1 to 55: Work 55 rows in g-st. Cast off in g-st.

FLYING HAT

Beg at lower edge using the long tail method and I, cast on 40 sts, RS facing to beg.
Rows 1 to 6: Beg with a k row, work 6 rows in st-st.
Row 7: (K2tog, k3) to end (32 sts).
Row 8 and foll 2 alt rows: Purl.
Row 9: (K2tog, k2) to end (24 sts).
Row 11: (K2tog, k1) to end (16 sts).
Row 13: (K2tog) to end (8 sts).
Thread yarn through sts on needle, pull tight and secure by threading yarn a second time through sts.

Ear flaps (make 2)

Using the long tail method and I, cast on 10 sts.
Row 1 (WS): K5, turn.
Row 2: S1k, k4.
Rows 3 and 4: Rep rows 1 and 2 once.
Cast off kwise.

MAKING UP

Note: Sew up all row-end seams on right side using mattress stitch one stitch in from the edge, unless otherwise stated; a one-stitch seam allowance has been allowed for this.

Shoes, legs, body, head, trousers, arms, hands, features and hair

Make up shoes, legs, body, head, trousers, arms, hands, work features and make up hair, as for Skateboarder on page 15.

Jacket

Sew up sleeve seams of jacket and sew across under arm. Place jacket on doll and sew up back seam. Place trim down centre front of jacket and sew all edges down.

Scarf

Fold scarf tails in half and sew fold to front of neck. Place neck piece around neck and sew up cast-on and cast-off stitches at back and sew all edges down.

Flying hat and goggles

Sew up row ends of flying hat and place on head. Sew lower edge of flying hat to head. Using picture as a guide and dark brown, embroider goggles using chain stitch, making two lines of stitches from side of hat around face to other side of hat, one line of stitches above and one line below eyes and join at middle.

Ear flaps

Sew wide row ends of ear flaps to lower edge of flying hat at both sides.

Clown

Materials

- Any DK (US: light worsted) yarn (amounts given are approximate):
  5g white (A)
  5g yellow (B)
  5g pale pink (C)
  5g green (D)
  5g petrol blue (E)
  5g red (F)
  2g bright pink (G)
  5g orange (H)
- Oddments of black and red for embroidery
- 1 pair of 3.25mm (UK10:US3) needles and a spare needle of the same size
- Knitters' pins and a blunt-ended needle for sewing up
- Tweezers (optional)
- Acrylic toy stuffing

Finished size

Clown stands 6¾in (17cm) tall

Tension

26 sts x 34 rows measure 4in (10cm) square over st-st using 3.25mm needles and DK yarn before stuffing

Abbreviations

See page 219

How to make Clown

LEGS, BODY AND HEAD
Right leg
Using the long tail method and A for leg, cast on 12 sts, WS facing to beg.
Rows 1 to 15: Beg with a p row, work 15 rows in st-st.
Break yarn and set aside.

Left leg
Work as for right leg but do not break yarn.

Join legs
Row 16: With RS facing, k across sts of left leg then with the same yarn cont k across sts of right leg (24 sts). Place a marker on first and last st of last row.
Rows 17 to 21: Beg with a p row, work 5 rows in st-st.
Rows 22 to 31: Change to B for upper body and work 10 rows in st-st.
Rows 32 and 33: Change to C for head and work 2 rows in st-st.
Row 34: K2, (m1, k4) to last 2 sts, m1, k2 (30 sts).
Rows 35 to 43: Beg with a p row, work 9 rows in st-st.
Row 44: (K2tog, k1) to end (20 sts).
Row 45: Purl.
Row 46: (K2tog) to end (10 sts).
Thread yarn through sts on needle and leave loose.

TROUSERS
Beg at centre back using the long tail method and D, cast on 11 sts and work in g-st, RS facing to beg.
Rows 1 to 28: Join on E and work 28 rows in g-st in stripes, carrying yarn loosely up side of work, taking yarn up WS without twisting it for a neat edge, and beg with 2 rows E then 2 rows D; do this alternately, finishing with 2 rows D.

Row 29: Using E, knit.
Row 30: Using E, cast off 4 sts and knit to end (7 sts).
Row 31: Using D, knit.
Row 32: Using D, cast on 4 sts at beg of next row using the knitting-on method and k this row (11 sts).
Rows 33 to 60: Work 28 rows in g-st in stripes, 2 rows E then 2 rows D and do this alternately, finishing with 2 rows D.
Row 61: Using E, knit.
Cast off using E in g-st.

SHOES (make 2)
Using the long tail method and F, cast on 14 sts, WS facing to beg.
Rows 1 to 9: Beg with a p row, work 9 rows in st-st.

Row 10: (K2tog) to end (7 sts).
Thread yarn through sts on needle, pull tight and secure by threading yarn a second time through sts.

SLEEVES AND HANDS
(make 2)
Make sleeves and hands using B for sleeves and C for hands, as for Doctor on page 61.

BRACES (make 2)
Using the long tail method and F, cast on 16 sts.
Row 1 (RS): Knit.
Cast off kwise.

BUTTONS (make 4)

Using the long tail method and G, cast on 10 sts.
Thread yarn through sts on needle, pull tight and secure by threading yarn a second time through sts.

NOSE

Using the long tail method and F, cast on 6 sts.
Thread yarn through sts on needle, pull tight and secure by threading yarn a second time through sts.

HAIR

Using the long tail method and H, cast on 6 sts and work in g-st, RS facing to beg.
Rows 1 to 49: Work 49 rows in g-st.
Cast off in g-st.

HAT

Using the long tail method and F, cast on 32 sts and beg in g-st, RS of brim facing to beg.
Rows 1 to 5: Work 5 rows in g-st.
Join on E for hat band and dec:
Row 6: (K2tog, k2) to end (24 sts).
Rows 7 to 11: Work 5 rows in g-st.
Rows 12 to 15: Cont in F and beg with a k row, work 4 rows in st-st.
Row 16: (K2tog, k1) to end (16 sts).
Row 17: Purl.
Row 18: (K2tog) to end (8 sts).
Thread yarn through sts on needle, pull tight and secure by threading yarn a second time through sts.

Flower

Using the long tail method and B, cast on 14 sts, WS facing to beg.
Rows 1 and 2: Change to A and p 1 row then k 1 row.
Row 3 (picot edge): P1, k1 (yrn, k2tog) to end.
Rows 4 and 5: K 1 row then p 1 row.

Row 6: (K2tog) to end (7 sts).
Thread yarn through sts on needle, pull tight and secure by threading yarn a second time through sts.

Stem

Using the long tail method and D, cast on 6 sts.
Cast off kwise.

MAKING UP

Note: Sew up all row-end seams on right side using mattress stitch one stitch in from the edge, unless otherwise stated; a one-stitch seam allowance has been allowed for this.

Legs, body and head

Sew up row ends of legs and bring markers together at crotch and sew round crotch. Stuff legs, leaving ankles open. Sew up row ends of body and head and stuff body and head. Pull stitches on a thread tight at top of head and fasten off. To shape neck, take a double piece of yarn to match body and sew a running stitch round last row of body at neck, sewing in and out of every half stitch. Pull tight, knot yarn and sew ends into neck.

Trousers

Oversew leg seams of trousers and oversew seam at centre back. Place trousers on doll and sew waist edge to first row of upper body all the way round.

Shoes

Sew up row ends of shoes and stuff shoes using tweezers or tip of scissors. Gather round cast-on stitches, pull tight and secure. Add more stuffing to ankles if needed. With toes pointing forwards, sew shoes to ankles.

Sleeves and hands

Make up sleeves and hands, as for Doctor on page 63.

Braces and buttons

Sew two ends of braces to front of trousers, take over shoulders and sew ends to back of trousers. Sew up row ends of buttons and sew four buttons to ends of braces at front and back.

Features

Mark position of eyes with two pins on 7th row above neck, spacing two knitted stitches apart. Embroider eyes in black (see page 218 for how to begin and fasten off the embroidery invisibly), making a small chain stitch beginning at marked position and ending on row above, and work a second chain stitch on top of first. Join row ends of nose and sew nose to row below eyes at centre front. Using picture as a guide, embroider mouth in red using two rows of back stitch close together.

Hair

Place hair around back of head and sew in place.

Hat and flower

Sew up row ends of hat and stuff top of hat lightly. Place hat on head and sew to head using back stitch at base of brim, sewing through hat to head. Gather round cast-on stitches of flower, pull tight and secure. Sew up row ends and fold along picot edge and stitch in place. Sew stalk to back of flower and sew flower and stalk to hat.

French Doll

Materials

♥ Any DK (US: light worsted) yarn
  (amounts given are approximate):
  5g black (A)
  5g pale pink (B)
  5g white (C)
  10g navy blue (D)
  5g brown (E)
  5g red (F)
♥ Oddments of black and red for embroidery
  and navy blue for making up
♥ 1 pair of 3.25mm (UK10:US3) needles and
  a spare needle of the same size
♥ Knitters' pins and a blunt-ended needle
  for sewing up
♥ Tweezers (optional)
♥ Acrylic toy stuffing
♥ A red pencil for shading cheeks

Finished size

French Doll stands 6in (15cm) tall

Tension

26 sts x 34 rows measure 4in (10cm)
square over st-st using 3.25mm needles
and DK yarn before stuffing

Abbreviations

See page 219

How to make French Doll

SHOES, LEGS, BODY, HEAD, TROUSERS, ARMS, HANDS AND HAIR

Make shoes, legs, body, head, trousers, arms, hands and hair using A for shoes, B for legs, C for lower body, D for upper body and B for head, make trousers in D, arms and hands in B and hair in E, as for Skateboarder on pages 13 and 14.

JUMPER

Note: Sleeves are worked first and knitted into body.

Sleeves (make 2)

Beg at cuff using the long tail method and D, cast on 16 sts, RS facing to beg.

Rows 1 and 2: P 1 row then k 1 row.
Rows 3 and 4: Join on C and k 1 row then p 1 row.
Work in stripes, carrying yarn loosely up side of work:

Rows 5 and 6: Using D, k 1 row then p 1 row.
Rows 7 and 8: Using C, k 1 row then p 1 row.
Rows 9 and 10: Using D, k 1 row then p 1 row.
Row 11: Using C, knit.
Row 12: Using C, cast off 3 sts pwise, p9, cast off rem 3 sts pwise and fasten off (10 sts).
Set aside.
Rep second sleeve as for first sleeve and set aside.

Front and back
Using the long tail method and D, cast on 38 sts, RS facing to beg.
Rows 1 and 2: P 1 row then k 1 row.
Rows 3 and 4: Join on C and k 1 row then p 1 row.
Work in stripes, carrying yarn loosely up side of work.
Rows 5 and 6: Join on D and k 1 row then p 1 row.
Rows 7 and 8: Using C, k 1 row then p 1 row.
Rows 9 and 10: Using D, k 1 row then p 1 row.
Row 11: Using C, knit.

Divide for armholes
Row 12: Using C, p8, cast off 4 sts pwise, p13, cast off 4 sts pwise, p7 (30 sts).

Join sleeves
Row 13: Using D and with RS of all pieces facing, k8 from left back, k10 from one sleeve, k14 across front, k10 from other sleeve, k8 from right back (50 sts).
Row 14: Using D, p6, (p2tog) twice, p6, (p2tog) twice, p10, (p2tog) twice, p6, (p2tog) twice, p6 (42 sts).
Row 15: Using C, k5, (k2tog) twice, k4,

(k2tog) twice, k8, (k2tog) twice, k4, (k2tog) twice, k5 (34 sts).
Row 16: Using C, purl.
Row 17: Using D, k4, (k2tog) twice, k2, (k2tog) twice, k6, (k2tog) twice, k2, (k2tog) twice, k4 (26 sts).
Row 18: Using D, k 1 row.
Cast off in D, pwise.

NECKERCHIEF
Make neckerchief in F, as for Cowboy on page 18.

BERET
Make beret in D, as for Artist on page 108.

MAKING UP
Note: Sew up all row-end seams on right side using mattress stitch one stitch in from the edge, unless otherwise stated; a one-stitch seam allowance has been allowed for this.

Shoes, legs, body, head, trousers, arms, hands, features and hair
Make up shoes, legs, body, head, trousers, arms, hands, work features and make up hair, as for Skateboarder on page 15.

Jumper
Make up jumper, as for Union Jack Doll on page 74.

Neckerchief
Make up neckerchief, as for Cowboy on page 19.

Beret
Make up beret, as for Artist on page 109.

Chef

Materials

- ♥ Any DK (US: light worsted) yarn (amounts given are approximate):
  10g black (A)
  5g pale pink (B)
  5g silver grey (C)
  15g white (D)
- ♥ Oddments of black, red and silver grey for embroidery
- ♥ 1 pair of 3.25mm (UK10:US3) needles and a spare needle of the same size
- ♥ Knitters' pins and a blunt-ended needle for sewing up
- ♥ Tweezers (optional)
- ♥ Acrylic toy stuffing
- ♥ A red pencil for shading cheeks

Finished size

Chef stands 7³/₄in (19.5cm) tall

Tension

26 sts x 34 rows measure 4in (10cm) square over st-st using 3.25mm needles and DK yarn before stuffing

Abbreviations

See page 219

How to make Chef

SHOES, LEGS, BODY AND HEAD

Make shoes, legs, body and head using A for shoes, B for legs, C for lower body, D for upper body and B for head, as for Skateboarder on page 13.

TROUSERS

First leg

Beg at lower edge using the long tail method and D, cast on 20 sts.
Row 1 (RS): Knit.
Row 2: K5, (m1, k5) to end (23 sts).
Join on A and work in patt:
Row 3: Using A, k1, (s1p, k1) to end.

Row 4: Using A, k1, (yf, s1p, yb, k1) to end.
Rows 5 and 6: Using D, work 2 rows in g-st.
Rows 7 to 22: Rep rows 3 to 6, 4 times more.
Row 23: Using A, cast off 2 sts, (s1p, k1) to end (21 sts).
Row 24: Using A, cast off 2 sts pwise, s1p, yb, k1, (yf, s1p, yb, k1) to end (19 sts).
Break yarn and set aside.

Second leg

Work second leg as for first leg but do not break yarn.

Join legs

Row 25: With RS facing, rejoin D and k across sts of second leg then with the same yarn cont k across sts of first leg (38 sts).
Row 26: Using D, k19, m1, k19 (39 sts).
Rows 27 to 34: Rep rows 3 to 6 twice more.
Cont in D and dec:
Row 35: K5, (k2tog, k7) 3 times, k2tog, k5 (35 sts).
Cast off kwise.

SLEEVES AND HANDS

Make sleeves and hands using D for sleeves and B for hands, as for Doctor on page 61.

123

HAIR

Make hair in A, as for Groom on page 48.

JACKET

Note: Sleeves are worked first and knitted into body.

Sleeves (make 2)

Beg at cuff using the long tail method and D, cast on 16 sts.
Row 1 (RS): Purl.
Rows 2 to 9: Beg with a p row, work 8 rows in st-st, finishing with a RS row.

Row 10: Cast off 3 sts pwise, p9, cast off rem 3 sts pwise and fasten off (10 sts).
Set aside.
Rep second sleeve as for first sleeve and set aside.

Front and back

Using the long tail method and D, cast on 48 sts, RS facing to beg.
Rows 1 and 2: P 2 rows.
Rows 3 to 5: Beg with a k row, work 3 rows in st-st and k the first st and last st on the p row, ending with a RS row.
Row 6: K1, p10, p2tog, p2, p2tog, p14, p2tog, p2, p2tog, p10, k1 (44 sts).
Rows 7 and 8: P 1 row then k 1 row.

Row 9: Knit.
Row 10: K1, p to last st, k1.
Rows 11 and 12: Rep rows 9 and 10 once.
Row 13: Knit.

Divide for armholes

Row 14: K1, p10, cast off 4 sts pwise, p13, cast off 4 sts pwise, p9, k1 (36 sts).

Join sleeves

Row 15: With RS of all pieces facing, k11 from right front, k10 from one sleeve, k14 across back, k10 from other sleeve, k11 from left front (56 sts).

Row 23: (K2tog) to end (8 sts). Thread yarn through sts on needle, pull tight and secure by threading yarn a second time through sts.

MAKING UP

Note: Sew up all row-end seams on right side using mattress stitch one stitch in from the edge, unless otherwise stated; a one-stitch seam allowance has been allowed for this.

Shoes, legs, body and head

Make up shoes, legs, body and head, as for Skateboarder on page 15.

Trousers

Sew up leg seams of trousers and sew round crotch. Sew up row ends at centre back and place trousers on doll. Sew cast-off stitches of trousers to first row of upper body all the way round.

Sleeves and hands

Make up sleeves and hands, as for Doctor on page 63.

Features and hair

Work features, as for Skateboarder on page 15. Make up hair, as for Groom on page 51.

Jacket and buttons

Sew up sleeve seams of jacket and sew across under arm. Place jacket on doll and overlap double-breasted front and sew in place. Sew collar to neck of doll. Using picture as a guide, embroider buttons in silver grey, making two small stitches close together for each button.

Hat

Sew up row ends of hat, stuff top of hat and lightly stuff narrow part. Pin and sew lower edge of hat to head.

Row 16: K1, p8, (p2tog) twice, p6, (p2tog) twice, p10, (p2tog) twice, p6, (p2tog) twice, p8, k1 (48 sts).
Row 17: K8, (k2tog) twice, k4, (k2tog) twice, k8, (k2tog) twice, k4, (k2tog) twice, k8, (40 sts).
Row 18: K1, p to last st, k1.
Row 19: K7, (k2tog) twice, k2, (k2tog) twice, k6, (k2tog) twice, k2, (k2tog) twice, k7 (32 sts).
Row 20: As row 18.

Work collar

Row 21: Purl.
Cast off kwise.

HAT

Using the long tail method and D, cast on 32 sts.
Row 1 (RS): Purl.
Rows 2 to 10: Beg with a p row, work 9 rows in st-st.
Row 11: K2, (m1, k4) to last 2 sts, m1, k2 (40 sts).
Rows 12 to 16: Beg with a p row, work 5 rows in st-st.
Row 17: (K2tog, k3) to end (32 sts).
Row 18 and foll 2 alt rows: Purl.
Row 19: (K2tog, k2) to end (24 sts).
Row 21: (K2tog, k1) to end (16 sts).

Farmer

Materials

- ♥ Any DK (US: light worsted) yarn (amounts given are approximate):
  5g dark brown (A)
  5g pale pink (B)
  5g white (C)
  5g green (D)
  5g denim blue (E)
  5g brown (F)
  5g grey (G)
  5g black (H)
  5g beige (I)
- ♥ Oddments of black and red for embroidery
- ♥ 1 pair of 3.25mm (UK10:US3) needles and a spare needle of the same size
- ♥ Knitters' pins and a blunt-ended needle for sewing up
- ♥ Tweezers (optional)
- ♥ Acrylic toy stuffing
- ♥ 1 plastic drinking straw (³/₁₆in/5mm diameter)
- ♥ 1 chenille stem
- ♥ A red pencil for shading cheeks

Finished size

Farmer stands 6in (15cm) tall

Tension

26 sts x 34 rows measure 4in (10cm) square over st-st using 3.25mm needles and DK yarn before stuffing

Abbreviations

See page 219

How to make Farmer

SHOES, LEGS, BODY AND HEAD

Make shoes, legs, body and head using A for shoes, B for legs, C for lower body, D for upper body and B for head, as for Skateboarder on page 13.

TROUSERS AND BELT

Make trousers and belt using E for trousers and A for belt, as for Cowboy on page 18.

SLEEVES, ARMS, HANDS AND ARM CUFFS

Make sleeves, arms, hands and arm cuffs using D for sleeves, B for arms and hands and D for arm cuffs, as for Painter & Decorator on page 29.

HAIR

Make hair in F, as for Skateboarder on page 14.

CAP

Make cap in G, as for Painter & Decorator on page 30.

LAMB
Body

Using the long tail method and C, cast on 16 sts and work in rev st-st.
Row 1 (RS): Purl.
Row 2: (K1, m1, k6, m1, k1) twice (20 sts).
Rows 3 to 9: Beg with a p row, work 7 rows in st-st.

Row 10: (K1, k2tog, k4, k2tog, k1) twice (16 sts).
Cast off pwise.

Head

Beg at top edge using the long tail method and H, cast on 8 sts and beg in rev st-st.
Row 1 (RS): Purl.
Row 2: K1, (m1, k1) to end (15 sts).
Rows 3 and 4: P 1 row then k 1 row. Change to C and continue in st-st.
Row 5: (K1 tbl) to end.
Rows 6 to 8: Beg with a p row, work 3 rows in st-st.
Row 9: (K2tog, k1) to end (10 sts).
Row 10: Purl.
Row 11: (K2tog) to end (5 sts).
Thread yarn through sts on needle, pull tight and secure by threading yarn a second time through sts.

Legs (make 4)

Beg at top edge using the long tail method and H, cast on 5 sts, WS facing to beg.
Rows 1 to 3: Beg with a p row, work 3 rows in st-st.
Cast off.

Ears (make 2)

Using the long tail method and H, cast on 3 sts.
Row 1: Knit.
Cast off kwise.

Tail

Using the long tail method and H, cast on 6 sts.
Row 1: K2, (kfb) twice, k2 (8 sts).
Cast off kwise.

CROOK

Using the long tail method and I, cast on 6 sts, WS facing to beg.
Beg with a p row, work in st-st for 6¾in (17cm).
Thread yarn through sts on needle, pull tight and secure by threading yarn a second time through sts.

MAKING UP

Note: Sew up all row-end seams on right side using mattress stitch one stitch in from the edge, unless otherwise stated; a one-stitch seam allowance has been allowed for this.

Shoes, legs, body and head

Make up shoes, legs, body and head, as for Skateboarder on page 15.

Trousers and belt

Make up trousers and belt, as for Cowboy on page 19.

Sleeves, arms, hands, arm cuffs and cap

Make up sleeves, arms, hands, arm cuffs and cap, as for Painter & Decorator on page 31.

Features and hair

Work features and make up hair, as for Skateboarder on page 15.

Lamb

Fold cast-on stitches of body in half and over-sew. Fold cast-off stitches in half and oversew. Stuff body and sew up row ends. Sew body of lamb to Farmer with Farmer's arm round lamb. Sew up row ends of white part of head and stuff. Sew up remaining row ends and with this seam at centre back, over-sew top edge. Sew head to body. Oversew cast-on and cast-off stitches of legs along length of legs and sew legs to body. Sew both ears to head at each side. Make a twist in tail and catch in place. Sew end of tail to lamb. Using black, embroider eyes, making a small vertical stitch for each eye on white part of head. Embroider nose and mouth in black, working a V-shape for nose and a long stitch from nose to centre of underneath for mouth (See page 218 for how to begin and fasten off the embroidery invisibly.)

Crook

Cut a piece of plastic drinking straw 4¾in (12cm) long. Fold chenille stem in half and place ends of chenille stem inside top of straw with 1¾in (4.5cm) of chenille stem showing at top. Place crook around drinking straw and chenille stem and oversew row ends along its length, enclosing straw and chenille stem inside. Gather round cast-on stitches, pull tight and fasten off. Using picture as a guide, bend top of crook around. Sew crook to hand of doll.

Prince & Princess

Materials

♥ Any DK (US: light worsted) yarn (amounts given are approximate):
  10g navy blue (A)
  10g pale pink (B)
  5g white (C)
  10g petrol blue (D)
  5g gold (E)
  5g brown (F)
  10g red (G)
  5g cerise (H)
  5g lemon (I)
♥ Oddments of black, red and gold for embroidery
♥ 1 pair of 3.25mm (UK10:US3) needles and a spare needle of the same size
♥ Knitters' pins and a blunt-ended needle for sewing up
♥ Tweezers (optional)
♥ Acrylic toy stuffing
♥ A red pencil for shading cheeks

Finished size

Prince & Princess stand 6¼in (16cm) tall

Tension

26 sts x 34 rows measure 4in (10cm) square over st-st using 3.25mm needles and DK yarn before stuffing

Abbreviations

See page 219

How to make Prince

BOOTS, LEGS, BODY AND HEAD
Right leg
Using the long tail method and A for boot, cast on 14 sts.

Place a marker on cast-on edge between the 5th and 6th st of the sts just cast on.

Row 1 (WS): Purl.

Row 2: K2, (m1, k2) to end (20 sts).

Rows 3 to 5: Beg with a p row, work 3 rows in st-st.

Row 6: K2, (k2tog) 6 times, k6 (14 sts).

Row 7: P7, p2tog, p1, p2tog, p2 (12 sts).

Rows 8 to 11: Work 4 rows in st-st.

Rows 12 to 21: Change to B for leg and work 10 rows in st-st.

Break yarn and set aside.

Left leg
Using the long tail method and A for boot, cast on 14 sts.

Place a marker on cast-on edge between the 9th and 10th st of the sts just cast on.

Row 1 (WS): Purl.

Row 2: K2, (m1, k2) to end (20 sts).

Rows 3 to 5: Beg with a p row, work 3 rows in st-st.

Row 6: K6, (k2tog) 6 times, k2 (14 sts).

Row 7: P2, p2tog, p1, p2tog, p7 (12 sts).

Rows 8 to 11: Work 4 rows in st-st.

Rows 12 to 21: Change to B for leg and work 10 rows in st-st.

Join legs
Row 22: Change to C for lower body and with RS facing, k across sts of left leg then with the same yarn cont k across sts of right leg (24 sts).

Rows 23 to 27: Beg with a p row, work 5 rows in st-st.

Rows 28 to 37: Change to D for upper body and work 10 rows in st-st.

Rows 38 and 39: Change to B for head and work 2 rows in st-st.

Row 40: K2, (m1, k4) to last 2 sts, m1, k2 (30 sts).

Rows 41 to 49: Beg with a p row, work 9 rows in st-st.

Row 50: (K2tog, k1) to end (20 sts).

Row 51: Purl.

Row 52: (K2tog) to end (10 sts). Thread yarn through sts on needle and leave loose.

BREECHES
First leg
Beg at lower edge using the long tail method and D, cast on 21 sts, WS facing to beg.

Rows 1 to 7: Beg with a p row, work 7 rows in st-st.

Rows 8 and 9: Cast off 2 sts at beg of next 2 rows (17 sts). Break yarn and set aside.

Second leg
Work second leg as for first leg but do not break yarn.

Join legs
Row 10: With RS facing, k across sts of second leg then with the same yarn cont k across sts of first leg (34 sts).

Rows 11 to 15: Beg with a p row, work 5 rows in st-st. Cast off.

BOOT TOPS (make 2)

Using the long tail method and A, cast on 20 sts, RS facing to beg. Cast off kwise.

ARMS AND HANDS

Make arms and hands in B, as for Skateboarder on pages 13 and 14.

JACKET

Note: Sleeves are worked first and knitted into body.

Sleeves (make 2)

Beg at cuff using the long tail method and D, cast on 16 sts, RS facing to beg.
Rows 1 and 2: P 2 rows.
Rows 3 and 4: Using E, work 2 rows in g-st.
Rows 5 to 9: Cont in D and beg with a k row, work 5 rows in st-st, finishing with a RS row.

Row 10: Cast off 3 sts pwise, p9, cast off rem 3 sts pwise and fasten off (10 sts).
Set aside.
Rep second sleeve as for first sleeve and set aside.

Front and back

Using the long tail method and D, cast on 42 sts, RS facing to beg.
Rows 1 and 2: P 2 rows.
Rows 3 to 6: Join on E and work 4 rows in g-st.
Rows 7 to 12: Cont in D and beg with a k row, work 6 rows in st-st and k the first 2 and last 2 sts on every p row.
Row 13: K8, k2tog, k2, k2tog, k14, k2tog, k2, k2tog, k8 (38 sts).

Divide for armholes

Row 14: K2, p6, cast off 4 sts pwise, p13, cast off 4 sts pwise, p5, k2 (30 sts).

Join sleeves

Row 15: With RS of all pieces facing, k8 from right front, k10 from one sleeve, k14 across back, k10 from other sleeve, k8 from left front (50 sts).
Row 16: K2, p4, (p2tog) twice, p6, (p2tog) twice, p10, (p2tog) twice, p6, (p2tog) twice, p4, k2 (42 sts).
Row 17: K5, (k2tog) twice, k4, (k2tog) twice, k8, (k2tog) twice, k4, (k2tog) twice, k5, (34 sts).
Row 18: K2, p to last 2 sts, k2.
Row 19: K4, (k2tog) twice, k2, (k2tog) twice, k6, (k2tog) twice, k2, (k2tog) twice, k4 (26 sts).
Row 20: K2, p to last 2 sts, k2.

Work collar

Rows 21 and 22: Work 2 rows in g-st. Cast off pwise.

HAIR

Make hair in F, as for Groom on page 48.

TIARA

Using the long tail method and E, cast on 12 sts.
Row 1 (WS): Purl.
Row 2: K9, turn.
Row 3: S1p, p5, turn.
Row 4: S1k, k to end.
Row 5 (picot edge): P1, k1, (yrn, k2tog) to end.
Rows 6 to 8: Rep rows 2 to 4 once.
Row 9: Purl.
Cast off.

CLOAK

Using the long tail method and G, cast on 34 sts and work in g-st, RS facing to beg.
Rows 1 to 10: Work 10 rows in g-st.
Row 11: (K2, k2tog) twice, k18, (k2, k2tog) twice (30 sts).
Rows 12 to 20: Work 9 rows in g-st.
Row 21: (K2, k2tog) twice, k14, (k2, k2tog) twice (26 sts).
Rows 22 to 30: Work 9 rows in st-st.

Row 31: (K2, k2tog) twice, k10, (k2, k2tog) twice (22 sts).
Rows 32 to 40: Work 9 rows in st-st.
Row 41: K1, k2tog, k16, k2tog, k1 (20 sts).
Cast off in g-st.

Cloak collar

Using the long tail method and G, cast on 22 sts and work in g-st.
Row 1 (RS): Knit.
Row 2: K2, k2tog, k14, k2tog, k2 (20 sts).
Cast off in g-st.

MAKING UP

Note: Sew up all row-end seams on right side using mattress stitch one stitch in from the edge, unless otherwise stated; a one-stitch seam allowance has been allowed for this.

Boots, legs, body and head

Make up boots, legs, body and head, as for Cowboy on page 19.

Breeches

Sew up leg seams of breeches and sew round crotch. Sew up row ends at centre back and place breeches on doll. Sew cast-off stitches of breeches to first row of upper body all the way round, and sew cast-on stitches of each leg to last row of boot.

Boot tops

Place boot tops around top of boots and sew up row ends, then sew boot tops to top of boots using back stitch all the way round.

Arms, hands and features

Make up arms and hands and work features, as for Skateboarder on page 15.

Jacket and buttons

Sew up sleeve seams of jacket and sew across underarm. Place jacket on doll and sew up centre front of jacket. Using picture as a guide, embroider buttons in gold down both sides of jacket front, making two small stitches close together for each button and a straight stitch to join each pair.

Hair

Make up hair, as for Groom on page 51.

Tiara

Bring cast-on and cast-off edges of tiara together and oversew. Sew tiara to top of head.

Cloak

Sew cast-off stitches of cloak to base of jacket collar at back. Sew on lower edge of cloak collar.

How to make Princess

SLIPPERS, LEGS, BODY AND HEAD

Right leg

Using the long tail method and H for slipper, cast on 14 sts.

Place a marker on cast-on edge between the 5th and 6th st of the sts just cast on.

Row 1 (WS): Purl.

Row 2: K2, (m1, k2) to end (20 sts).

Rows 3 and 4: P 1 row then k 1 row.

Row 5: Change to B for leg and p 1 row.

Row 6: K2, (k2tog) 6 times, k6 (14 sts).

Row 7: P7, p2tog, p1, p2tog, p2 (12 sts).

Rows 8 to 21: Work 14 rows in st-st. Break yarn and set aside.

Left leg

Using the long tail method and H for slipper, cast on 14 sts.

Place a marker on cast-on edge between the 9th and 10th st of the sts just cast on.

Row 1 (WS): Purl.

Row 2: K2, (m1, k2) to end (20 sts).

Rows 3 and 4: P 1 row then k 1 row.

Row 5: Change to B for leg and p 1 row.

Row 6: K6, (k2tog) 6 times, k2 (14 sts).

Row 7: P2, p2tog, p1, p2tog, p7 (12 sts).

Rows 8 to 21: Work 14 rows in st-st.

Join legs

Row 22: Change to C for lower body and with RS facing, k across sts of left leg then with the same yarn cont k across sts of right leg (24 sts).

Rows 23 to 26: Beg with a p row, work 4 rows in st-st, ending with a RS row.

Rows 27 to 33: Change to H for upper body and beg with a P row, work 7 rows in st-st.

Rows 34 to 37: Change to B for neck and work 4 rows in st-st.

Place a marker on last row for neck gathering.

Rows 38 and 39: Work 2 rows in st-st.

Row 40: K2, (m1, k4) to last 2 sts, m1, k2 (30 sts).
Rows 41 to 49: Beg with a p row, work 9 rows in st-st.
Row 50: (K2tog, k1) to end (20 sts).
Row 51: Purl.
Row 52: (K2tog) to end (10 sts). Thread yarn through sts on needle and leave loose.

SKIRT
Using the long tail method and C, cast on 40 sts, WS facing to beg.
Rows 1 and 2: P 1 row then k 1 row (this part is turned under).
Row 3 (picot edge): P1, k1, (yrn, k2tog) to end.
Rows 4 and 5: K 1 row then p 1 row.
Rows 6 and 7: Change to H and work 2 rows in g-st.
Rows 8 to 23: Beg with a k row, work 16 rows in st-st.
Row 24: (K2tog, k3) to end (32 sts).
Row 25: Purl.
Row 26: (K2tog, k2) to end (24 sts). Cast off pwise.

SASH
Using the long tail method and D, cast on 31 sts.
Row 1 (RS): K14, k3tog, k14 (29 sts). Cast off kwise.

ARMS AND HANDS
Make arms and hands in B, as for Ballerina on page 34.

NECK EDGING
Using the long tail method and C, cast on 30 sts, WS facing to beg.
Row 1: Purl.
Row 2 (picot edge): K2, (yrn, k2tog) to end.
Row 3: Purl.
Cast off.

HAIR
Make hair in I, as for Valentine on page 22.

Hair locks (make 2)
Using the long tail method and I, cast on 12 sts and work in g-st, RS facing to beg.
Rows 1 to 4: Work 4 rows in g-st.
Row 5: (K2tog, k1) to end (8 sts).
Row 6: Knit.
Row 7: (K2tog) to end (4 sts).
Row 8: Knit.
Thread yarn through sts on needle, pull tight and secure by threading yarn a second time through sts.

TIARA
Make tiara in E, as for Prince.

CLOAK
Make cloak in A, as for Prince.

MAKING UP
Note: Sew up all row-end seams on right side using mattress stitch one stitch in from the edge, unless otherwise stated; a one-stitch seam allowance has been allowed for this.

Slippers, legs, body and head
Sew up row ends of slippers and ankles. With markers at tips of toes, oversew cast-on stitches; leg seam will be ¼in (6mm) on inside edge of heel. Place a ball of stuffing into toes. Sew up row ends of legs and sew round crotch. Stuff legs, sew up row ends of body and head, and stuff body and head. Pull stitches on a thread tight at top of head and fasten off. To shape neck, take a double length of pale pink yarn and sew a running stitch round row with marker at neck, sewing in and out of every half stitch. Pull tight, knot yarn and sew ends into neck. To shape waist, take a double length of yarn to match upper body and sew a running stitch around first row of upper body at waist. Pull waist in and knot yarn and sew ends into waist.

Skirt

Fold under lower edge of skirt and hem in place. Sew up row ends of skirt and place skirt on doll. Sew cast-off stitches of skirt to waist of doll all the way round.

Sash

Place sash around waist and oversew row ends at back. Sew all edges down.

Arms and hands

Make up arms and hands, as for Ballerina on page 35.

Neck edging

Fold neck edging along picot edge and oversew cast-on and cast-off stitches. Place neck edging around neck and join row ends at back. Pin and sew neck edging around top of dress.

Features, hair and hair locks

Work features, as for Skateboarder on page 15. Make up hair, as for Valentine on page 23. Oversew row ends of hair locks and sew to hair, one at each side.

Tiara and cloak

Make up tiara and cloak, as for Prince.

Footballer

Materials

- ♥ Any DK (US: light worsted) yarn (amounts given are approximate):
  5g black (A)
  5g medium blue (B)
  5g pale pink (C)
  5g white (D)
  5g brown (E)
- ♥ Oddments of black, red and grey for embroidery
- ♥ pair of 3.25mm (UK10:US3) needles and a spare needle of the same size
- ♥ Knitters' pins and a blunt-ended needle for sewing up
- ♥ Tweezers (optional)
- ♥ Acrylic toy stuffing
- ♥ A red pencil for shading cheeks

Finished size

Footballer stands 6in (15cm) tall

Tension

26 sts x 34 rows measure 4in (10cm) square over st-st using 3.25mm needles and DK yarn before stuffing

Abbreviations

See page 219

How to make Footballer

SHOES, SOCKS, LEGS, BODY AND HEAD
Right leg
Using the long tail method and A for shoe, cast on 14 sts.
Place a marker on cast-on edge between the 5th and 6th st of the sts just cast on.
Row 1 (WS): Purl.
Row 2: K2, (m1, k2) to end (20 sts).
Rows 3 to 5: Beg with a p row, work 3 rows in st-st.
Row 6: K2, (k2tog) 6 times, k6 (14 sts).
Change to B for sock and dec:
Row 7: P7, p2tog, p1, p2tog, p2 (12 sts).
Rows 8 to 11: Work 4 rows in st-st.
Rows 12 to 21: Change to C for leg and work 10 rows in st-st.
Break yarn and set aside.

Left leg
Using the long tail method and A for shoe, cast on 14 sts.
Place a marker on cast-on edge between the 9th and 10th st of the sts just cast on.
Row 1 (WS): Purl.
Row 2: K2, (m1, k2) to end (20 sts).
Rows 3 to 5: Beg with a p row, work 3 rows in st-st.
Row 6: K6, (k2tog) 6 times, k2 (14 sts).
Change to B for sock and dec:
Row 7: P2, p2tog, p1, p2tog, p7 (12 sts).
Rows 8 to 11: Work 4 rows in st-st.
Rows 12 to 21: Change to C for leg and work 10 rows in st-st.

Join legs
Row 22: Change to D for lower body and with RS facing, k across sts of left leg then with the same yarn cont k across sts of right leg (24 sts).
Rows 23 to 27: Beg with a p row, work 5 rows in st-st.
Rows 28 to 37: Change to C for upper body and work 10 rows in st-st.
Place a marker on last row for neck gathering.
Rows 38 and 39: Work 2 rows in st-st.
Row 40: K2, (m1, k4) to last 2 sts, m1, k2 (30 sts).
Rows 41 to 49: Beg with a p row, work 9 rows in st-st.
Row 50: (K2tog, k1) to end (20 sts).
Row 51: Purl.
Row 52: (K2tog) to end (10 sts).
Thread yarn through sts on needle and leave loose.

SHORTS
First leg
Beg at lower edge using the long tail method and D, cast on 21 sts and beg in g-st, RS facing to beg.
Rows 1 and 2: Join on B and work 2 rows in g-st.
Rows 3 and 4: Cont in D and beg with a k row, work 2 rows in st-st.
Rows 5 and 6: Cont in st-st and cast off 2 sts at beg of next 2 rows (17 sts).
Break yarn and set aside.

Second leg

Work second leg as for first leg but do not break yarn.

Join legs

Row 7: With RS facing, k across sts of second leg then with the same yarn cont k across sts of first leg (34 sts).
Rows 8 to 12: Beg with a p row, work 5 rows in st-st.
Cast off.

SOCK TOPS (make 2)

Using the long tail method and D, cast on 18 sts.
Cast off kwise.

ARMS AND HANDS

Make arms and hands in C, as for Ballerina on page 34.

FOOTBALL SHIRT

Note: Sleeves are worked first and knitted into body.

Sleeves (make 2)

Using the long tail method and B, cast on 16 sts, RS facing to beg.
Rows 1 to 3: Beg with a k row, work 3 rows in st-st, finishing with a RS row.
Row 4: Cast off 3 sts pwise, p9, cast off rem 3 sts pwise and fasten off (10 sts).
Set aside.

Rep second sleeve as for first sleeve and set aside.

Front and back

Using the long tail method and B, cast on 38 sts, RS facing to beg.
Rows 1 to 7: Beg with a k row, work 7 rows in st-st finishing with a RS row.

Divide for armholes

Row 8: P8, cast off 4 sts pwise, p13, cast off 4 sts pwise, p7 (30 sts).

Join sleeves

Row 9: With RS of all pieces facing, k8 from left back, k10 from one sleeve, k14 across front, k10 from other sleeve, k8 from right back (50 sts).
Row 10: P6, (p2tog) twice, p6, (p2tog) twice, p10, (p2tog) twice, p6, (p2tog) twice, p6 (42 sts).

Work left back and left front

Row 11: K5, (k2tog) twice, k4, (k2tog) twice, k2, k2tog tbl, turn and work on these 16 sts.
Row 12: Purl.
Row 13: K4, (k2tog) twice, k2, (k2tog) 3 times (11 sts).
Row 14: P2tog, p to end (10 sts).
Cast off.

Work right front and right back

Row 15: Rejoin yarn to rem sts and K2tog, k2, (k2tog) twice, k4, (k2tog) twice, k5 (16 sts).
Row 16: Purl.
Row 17: (K2tog) 3 times, k2, (k2tog) twice, k4 (11 sts).
Row 18: P to last 2 sts, p2tog (10 sts).
Cast off.

Collar

Using the long tail method and D, cast on 39 sts, RS facing to beg.
Row 1: K18, k3tog, k18 (37 sts).
Cast off kwise.

HAIR
Make hair in E, as for Skateboarder on page 14.

FOOTBALL
Using the long tail method and D, cast on 5 sts.
Row 1 (WS): Purl.
Row 2: K1, (m1, k1) to end (9 sts).
Rows 3 and 4: Rep row 1 and 2 once (17 sts).
Rows 5 to 11: Beg with a p row, work 7 rows in st-st.
Row 12: K2tog, (k1, k2tog) to end (11 sts).
Row 13: Purl.
Row 14: K2tog, (k1, k2tog) to end (7 sts).
Thread yarn through sts on needle, pull tight and secure by threading yarn a second time through sts.

MAKING UP
Note: Sew up all row-end seams on right side using mattress stitch one stitch in from the edge, unless otherwise stated; a one-stitch seam allowance has been allowed for this.

Shoes, legs, body, head and shorts
Make up shoes, legs, body, head and shorts, as for Tennis Player on page 55.

Sock tops
Place sock tops around tops of socks and oversew row ends then sew to legs all the way round.

Arms and hands
Make up arms and hands, as for Ballerina on page 35.

Football shirt
Sew up sleeve seams of football shirt and sew across under arm. Place football shirt on doll and sew up back seam. Place collar around neck and oversew row ends. Pin and sew collar to doll using back stitch down middle of band.

Features, hair and laces
Work features and make up hair, as for Skateboarder on page 15. Using picture as a guide and grey, embroider laces on shoes.

Football
Gather round cast-on stitches of football and sew up row ends leaving a gap, stuff and sew up gap. Using picture as a guide, embroider spots in black, making four stitches close together for each spot.

Fitness Instructor

Materials

- ♥ Any DK (US: light worsted) yarn
  (amounts given are approximate):
  5g silver grey (A)
  2g lime green (B)
  5g pale pink (C)
  5g black (D)
  5g cerise (E)
  10g lemon (F)
- ♥ Oddments of black and red for embroidery
  and lemon and lime green for making up
- ♥ 1 pair of 3.25mm (UK10:US3) needles and
  a spare needle of the same size
- ♥ Knitters' pins and a blunt-ended needle
  for sewing up
- ♥ Tweezers (optional)
- ♥ Acrylic toy stuffing
- ♥ A red pencil for shading cheeks

Finished size

Fitness Instructor stands 6in (15cm) tall

Tension

26 sts x 34 rows measure 4in (10cm)
square over st-st using 3.25mm needles
and DK yarn before stuffing

Abbreviations

See page 219

How to make Fitness Instructor

SHOES, SOCKS, LEGS, BODY AND HEAD

Right leg
Using the long tail method and A for shoe, cast on 14 sts.
Place a marker on cast-on edge between the 5th and 6th st of the sts just cast on.
Row 1 (WS): Purl.
Row 2: K2, (m1, k2) to end (20 sts).
Rows 3 to 5: Beg with a p row, work 3 rows in st-st.
Row 6: K2, (k2tog) 6 times, k6 (14 sts). Change to B for sock and dec:
Row 7: P7, p2tog, p1, p2tog, p2 (12 sts).
Row 8: Purl.

Rows 9 to 11: Change to C for leg and beg with a p row, work 3 rows in st-st.
Rows 12 and 13: Change to D for leggings and work 2 rows in g-st.
Rows 14 to 21: Beg with a k row, work 8 rows in st-st.
Break yarn and set aside.

Left leg
Using the long tail method and A for shoe, cast on 14 sts.
Place a marker on cast-on edge between the 9th and 10th st of the sts just cast on.
Row 1 (WS): Purl.
Row 2: K2, (m1, k2) to end (20 sts).

Rows 3 to 5: Beg with a p row, work 3 rows in st-st.
Row 6: K6, (k2tog) 6 times, k2 (14 sts). Change to B for sock and dec:
Row 7: P2, p2tog, p1, p2tog, p7 (12 sts).
Row 8: Purl.
Rows 9 to 11: Change to C for leg and beg with a p row, work 3 rows in st-st.
Rows 12 and 13: Change to D for leggings and work 2 row in g-st.
Rows 14 to 21: Beg with a k row, work 8 rows in st-st.

Join legs
Row 22: With RS facing, k across sts of left leg then with the same yarn cont k across sts of right leg (24 sts).

143

Place a marker on first and last st of last row.
Rows 23 to 33: Beg with a p row, work 11 rows in st-st.
Rows 34 to 37: Change to C for upper body and work 4 rows in st-st.
Place a marker on last row for neck gathering.
Rows 38 and 39: Work 2 rows in st-st.
Row 40: K2, (m1, k4) to last 2 sts, m1, k2 (30 sts).
Rows 41 to 49: Beg with a p row, work 9 rows in st-st.
Row 50: (K2tog, k1) to end (20 sts).
Row 51: Purl.
Row 52: (K2tog) to end (10 sts).
Thread yarn through sts on needle and leave loose.

LEOTARD
Beg at front using the long tail method and E, cast on 17 sts, WS facing to beg.
Rows 1 to 7: Beg with a p row, work 7 rows in st-st.
Row 8: K2tog, k to last 2 sts, k2tog (15 sts).
Row 9: P2tog, p to last 2 sts, p2tog (13 sts).
Rows 10 to 13: Rep rows 8 and 9 twice more (5 sts).
Row 14: K2tog, k1, k2tog (3 sts).
Rows 15 to 19: Beg with a p row, work 5 rows in st-st.
Row 20: K1, (m1, k1) twice (5 sts).
Row 21 and foll alt row: Purl.
Row 22: K1, (m1, k1) to end (9 sts).
Row 24: (K1, m1) twice, k to last 2 sts, (m1, k1) twice (13 sts).
Row 25: Purl.
Row 26: As row 24 (17 sts).

Rows 27 to 33: Beg with a p row, work 7 rows in st-st.
Cast off.

ARMS AND HANDS
Make arms and hands in C, as for Ballerina on page 34.

NECK EDGING
Using the long tail method and E, cast on 36 sts, RS facing to beg.
Cast off pwise.

HAIR
Make hair in F, as for Valentine on page 22.

MAKING UP

Note: Sew up all row-end seams on right side using mattress stitch one stitch in from the edge, unless otherwise stated; a one-stitch seam allowance has been allowed for this.

Shoes, socks, legs, body and head

Sew up row ends of shoes and socks. With markers at tips of toes, oversew cast-on stitches; leg seam will be ¼in (6mm) on inside edge of heel. Place a ball of stuffing into toes and sew up row ends of legs. Bring markers together at crotch and sew round crotch. Stuff legs, sew up row ends of body and head, and stuff body and head. Pull stitches on a thread tight at top of head and fasten off. To shape neck, take a double piece of pale pink yarn and sew a running stitch round row with marker at neck, sewing in and out of every half stitch. Pull tight, knot yarn and sew ends into neck.

Leotard

Sew up row ends of leotard and place on doll. Sew cast-on and cast-off stitches to body all the way round.

Arms, hands and neck edging

Make up arms, hands and neck edging, as for Ballerina on page 35.

Features

Work features, as for Skateboarder on page 15.

Hair and bunches

Make up hair, as for Valentine on page 23. To make bunches, wind lemon around four fingers 30 times and cut through all loops. Lay 30 strands flat and tie tightly at middle and fold in half. Repeat for second bunch and sew bunches to sides of head. Trim ends of bunches. Wind lime green around base of bunches and tie and run ends into head.

Athlete

Materials

- Any DK (US: light worsted) yarn
  (amounts given are approximate):
  5g florescent green (A)
  5g white (B)
  5g pale pink (C)
  5g navy blue (D)
  5g orange (E)
  5g brown (f)
- Oddments of black and red for embroidery
- 1 pair of 3.25mm (UK10:US3) needles and
  a spare needle of the same size
- Knitters' pins and a blunt-ended needle
  for sewing up
- Tweezers (optional)
- Acrylic toy stuffing
- A red pencil for shading cheeks

Finished size

Athlete stands 6in (15cm) tall

Tension

26 sts x 34 rows measure 4in (10cm)
square over st-st using 3.25mm needles
and DK yarn before stuffing

Abbreviations

See page 219

How to make Athlete

SHOES, SOCKS, LEGS, BODY AND HEAD
Right leg
Using the long tail method and A for shoe, cast on 14 sts.

Place a marker on cast-on edge between the 5th and 6th st of the sts just cast on.

Row 1 (WS): Purl.

Row 2: K2, (m1, k2) to end (20 sts).

Rows 3 to 5: Beg with a p row, work 3 rows in st-st.

Row 6: K2, (k2tog) 6 times, k6 (14 sts). Change to B for sock and dec:

Row 7: P7, p2tog, p1, p2tog, p2 (12 sts).

Rows 8 and 9: Work 2 rows in g-st.

Rows 10 to 21: Change to C for leg and beg with a k row, work 12 rows in st-st.

Break yarn and set aside.

Left leg
Using the long tail method and A for shoe, cast on 14 sts.

Place a marker on cast-on edge between the 9th and 10th st of the sts just cast on.

Row 1 (WS): Purl.

Row 2: K2, (m1, k2) to end (20 sts).

Rows 3 to 5: Beg with a p row, work 3 rows in st-st.

Row 6: K6, (k2tog) 6 times, k2 (14 sts). Change to B for sock and dec:

Row 7: P2, p2tog, p1, p2tog, p7 (12 sts).

Rows 8 and 9: Work 2 rows in g-st.

Rows 10 to 21: Change to C for leg and beg with a k row, work 12 rows in st-st.

Join legs
Row 22: Change to D for lower body and with RS facing, k across sts of left leg then with the same yarn cont k across sts of right leg (24 sts).

Rows 23 to 27: Beg with a p row, work 5 rows in st-st.

Rows 28 to 33: Change to B for upper body and work 6 rows in st-st.

Rows 34 to 37: Change to C and work 4 rows in st-st.
Place a marker on last row for neck gathering.
Rows 38 and 39: Work 2 rows in st-st.
Row 40: K2, (m1, k4) to last 2 sts, m1, k2 (30 sts).
Rows 41 to 49: Beg with a p row, work 9 rows in st-st.

Row 50: (K2tog, k1) to end (20 sts).
Row 51: Purl.
Row 52: (K2tog) to end (10 sts).
Thread yarn through sts on needle and leave loose.

SHORTS

Make shorts in D, as for Tennis Player on page 53.

SPORTS VEST

Using the long tail method and B, cast on 38 sts.
Row 1 (RS): Purl.
Rows 2 to 4: Beg with a p row, work 3 rows in st-st.
Join on colours as required:
Row 5: Using D, knit.
Rows 6 and 7: Using E, p 1 row then k 1 row.
Row 8: Using D, purl.
Rows 9 to 11: Cont in B and beg with a k row, work 3 rows in st-st ending with a RS row.
Row 12: P3, (p2tog, p3) to end (31 sts).
Cast off.

ARMS AND HANDS

Make arms and hands in C, as for Ballerina on page 34.

NECK EDGING

Make neck edging in E, as for Fitness Instructor on page 144.

HAIR

Make hair in F, as for Skateboarder on page 14.

MAKING UP

Note: Sew up all row-end seams on right side using mattress stitch one stitch in from the edge, unless otherwise stated; a one-stitch seam allowance has been allowed for this.

Shoes, legs, body, head and shorts

Make up shoes, legs, body, head and shorts, as for Tennis Player on page 55.

Sports vest

Place sports vest around doll and sew up row ends at centre back. Sew cast-off stitches to last row of upper body all the way round.

Arms, hands and neck edging

Make up arms, hands and neck edging, as for Ballerina on page 35.

Features, hair and embroidery

Work features and make up hair, as for Skateboarder on page 15. Using black, embroider a stripe on both shoes.

Scotsman with Bagpipes

Materials

- ♥ Any DK (US: light worsted) yarn
  (amounts given are approximate):
  5g black (A)
  5g khaki green (B)
  5g pale pink (C)
  5g white (D)
  5g lemon (E)
  5g mustard (F)
  5g classic red (G)
  5g brown (H)
  5g denim blue (I)
  5g cherry red (J)
  2g cream (K)
- ♥ Oddments of black, red and mustard for
  embroidery and black and red for making up
- ♥ 1 pair of 3.25mm (UK10:US3) needles and
  a spare needle of the same size
- ♥ Knitters' pins and a blunt-ended needle for
  sewing up
- ♥ Tweezers (optional)
- ♥ Acrylic toy stuffing
- ♥ 4 plastic drinking straws
  (¹⁄₁₆in/5mm diameter)
- ♥ A red pencil for shading cheeks

Finished size

Scotsman with Bagpipes stands
6in (15cm) tall

Tension

26 sts x 34 rows measure 4in (10cm)
square over st-st using 3.25mm needles
and DK yarn before stuffing

Abbreviations

See page 219

How to make Scotsman with Bagpipes

SHOES, SOCKS, LEGS, BODY AND HEAD
Right leg
Using the long tail method and A for shoe, cast on 14 sts.
Place a marker on cast-on edge between the 5th and 6th st of the sts just cast on.
Row 1 (WS): Purl.
Row 2: K2, (m1, k2) to end (20 sts).
Rows 3 to 5: Beg with a p row, work 3 rows in st-st.
Row 6: K2, (k2tog) 6 times, k6 (14 sts).
Change to B for sock and dec:
Row 7: P7, p2tog, p1, p2tog, p2 (12 sts).
Rows 8 and 9: Work 2 rows in st-st.
Rows 10 to 21: Change to C for leg and work 12 rows in st-st.
Break yarn and set aside.

Left leg
Using the long tail method and A for shoe, cast on 14 sts.
Place a marker on cast-on edge between the 9th and 10th st of the sts just cast on.
Row 1 (WS): Purl.
Row 2: K2, (m1, k2) to end (20 sts).
Rows 3 to 5: Beg with a p row, work 3 rows in st-st.
Row 6: K6, (k2tog) 6 times, k2 (14 sts).
Change to B for sock and dec:
Row 7: P2, p2tog, p1, p2tog, p7 (12 sts).
Rows 8 and 9: Work 2 rows in st-st.
Rows 10 to 21: Change to C for leg and work 12 rows in st-st.

Join legs
Row 22: Using D, and with RS facing, k across sts of left leg then with the same yarn cont k across sts of right leg (24 sts).
Rows 23 to 27: Beg with a p row, work 5 rows in st-st.

Rows 28 to 37: Change to E for upper body and work 10 rows in st-st.
Rows 38 and 39: Change to C for head and work 2 rows in st-st.
Row 40: K2, (m1, k4) to last 2 sts, m1, k2 (30 sts).
Rows 41 to 49: Beg with a p row, work 9 rows in st-st.
Row 50: (K2tog, k1) to end (20 sts).
Row 51: Purl.
Row 52: (K2tog) to end (10 sts).
Thread yarn through sts on needle and leave loose.

SOCK TOPS
Make sock tops in B, as for Footballer on page 140.

KILT
Using the long tail method and F, cast on 58 sts.
Join on G and work in stripes patt and rejoin F as required and carry G loosely up side of work:
Row 1 (RS): Using G, k4, (p1, k4) twice, (p2, k2) to end.
Row 2: Using G, (p2, k2) 11 times, (p4, k1) twice, p2, k2.
Rows 3 and 4: Using G, rep rows 1 and 2 once.
Rows 5 and 6: Using F, rep rows 1 and 2 once.
Rows 7 to 10: Using G, rep rows 1 to 4 once.
Row 11: Using F, as row 1.
Row 12: Using F, (p2, k2tog) 11 times, (p4, k1) twice, p2, k2 (47 sts).
Cast off kwise using F.

SLEEVES AND HANDS
(make 2)
Beg at shoulder using the long tail
method and E, cast on 4 sts.
Row 1 (WS): Purl.
Row 2: K1, (m1, k1) to end (7 sts).
Row 3: Purl.
Row 4: K1, m1, k to last st, m1, k1
(9 sts).
Rows 5 and 6: Rep rows 3 and 4
once (11 sts).
Rows 7 to 16: Beg with a p row,
work 10 rows in st-st, finishing with
a RS row.
Rows 17 to 19: Change to C for hand
and beg with a p row, work 3 rows
in st-st.
Row 20: K2tog, (k1, k2tog) to end
(7 sts).
Thread yarn through sts on needle,
pull tight and secure by threading
yarn a second time through sts.

CUFFS
Make cuffs in E, as for Cowboy on
page 18.

HAIR
Make hair in H, as for Groom on
page 48.

BERET
Make beret in J, as for Artist on
page 108.

SPORRAN
Using the long tail method and D,
cast on 6 sts and work in g-st, RS
facing to beg.
Rows 1 and 2: Work 2 rows in g-st.
Row 3: K2tog, k2, k2tog (4 sts).
Row 4: Knit.
Row 5: K1, k2tog, k1 (3 sts).
Cast off in g-st.

BAGPIPES
Bag
Using the long tail method and J, cast
on 15 sts, WS facing to beg.
Rows 1 to 11: Beg with a p row, work
11 rows in st-st.
Row 12: K5, k2tog, k1, k2tog, k5
(13 sts).
Rows 13 to 15: Beg with a p row,
work 3 rows in st-st.
Row 16: K4, k2tog, k1, k2tog, k4
(11 sts).
Row 17: Purl.
Row 18: K3, k2tog, k1, k2tog, k3 (9 sts).
Row 19: Purl.
Cast off.

Pipes
Make 1 long pipe and using the
thumb method and A, cast on 6 sts,
WS facing to beg.
Beg with a p row, work in st-st for
3½in (9cm).
Cast off.
Make 2 short pipes as for long pipe
and work in st-st for 3in (7.5cm).

and oversew row ends. Sew cuffs to wrists all the way round. Leaving armholes open, sew arms to body, sewing top of arms to second row below neck at each side and sloping the arms forward.

Features and hair
Work features, as for Skateboarder on page 15. Make up hair, as for Groom on page 51.

Beret
Make up beret, as for Artist on page 109.

Sporran
Make a single small fringe on centre front of purse in black yarn and trim ends. Make a twisted cord (see page 218) using one strand of black yarn, beginning with the yarn 24in (60cm) long. Fold twisted cord in half and tie a knot 3½in (9cm) from folded end and trim ends. Place twisted cord around waist with knot below and sew sporran over knot to hide knot. Sew twisted cord to waist at back.

Bagpipes
Fold cast-on and cast-off stitches of bag in half and oversew. Sew up row ends, leaving a gap, stuff and sew up gap. Sew bag to front of doll. Cut a piece of plastic drinking straw 3in (7.5cm) long for long pipe, two pieces each 2½in (6.5cm) long for short pipes, one piece ¾in (2cm) long for blowpipe and one piece 1¼in (3cm) long for finger pipe. Place knitting around straws and sew up row ends along length, enclosing straws inside. Using picture as a guide, place trim around straws and oversew row ends. Sew trim in place. Sew three pipes, blowpipe and finger pipe to bag then sew blowpipe to mouth and hands to finger pipe. Make a plaited cord in red for trim, 4in (10cm) long. Knot and trim ends and sew to top of pipes.

Blowpipe and finger pipe
Make blowpipe as for long pipe working in st-st for 1¼in (3cm). Make finger pipe as for long pipe working in st-st for 1¾in (4.5cm).

Trim (make 8 pieces)
Using the long tail method and K, cast on 12 sts.
Cast off kwise.

MAKING UP
Note: Sew up all row-end seams on right side using mattress stitch one stitch in from the edge, unless otherwise stated; a one-stitch seam allowance has been allowed for this.

Shoes, socks, legs, body and head
Sew up row ends of shoes. With markers at tips of toes, oversew cast-on stitches; leg seam will be ¼in (6mm) on inside edge of heel. Place a ball of stuffing into toes, sew up row ends of socks and legs and sew round crotch. Stuff legs, sew up row ends of body and head, and stuff body and head. Pull stitches on a thread tight at top of head and fasten off. To shape neck, take a double piece of yarn to match body and sew a running stitch round last row of body at neck, sewing in and out of every half stitch. Pull tight, knot yarn and sew ends into neck.

Sock tops
Make up sock tops, as for Footballer on page 141.

Kilt
Embroider two vertical lines of chain stitch at front of skirt on lines of purl stitches. Place kilt around waist and overlap front. Sew around waist.

Sleeves, hands and cuffs
Sew up straight row ends of sleeves from fingers to underarm and stuff arms using tweezers or tip of scissors. Place cuffs around wrists

Santa & Mrs Claus

Materials

- ♥ Any DK (US: light worsted) yarn
  (amounts given are approximate):
  5g black (A)
  20g red (B)
  5g pale pink (C)
  10g white (D)
- ♥ Oddments of black, red, gold and green for
  embroidery and red and white for making up
- ♥ 1 pair of 3.25mm (UK10:US3) needles and
  a spare needle of the same size
- ♥ Knitters' pins and a blunt-ended needle
  for sewing up
- ♥ Tweezers (optional)
- ♥ Acrylic toy stuffing
- ♥ A red pencil for shading cheeks

Finished size

Santa stands 6½in (16.5cm) tall
Mrs Claus stands 6½in (16.5cm) tall

Tension

26 sts x 34 rows measure 4in (10cm)
square over st-st using 3.25mm needles
and DK yarn before stuffing

Abbreviations

See page 219

How to make Santa

BOOTS, LEGS, BODY AND HEAD

Right leg

Using the long tail method and A for boot, cast on 18 sts.

Place a marker on cast-on edge between the 7th and 8th st of the sts just cast on.

Row 1 (WS): Purl.

Row 2: K2, (m1, k2) to end (26 sts).

Rows 3 to 7: Beg with a p row, work 5 rows in st-st.

Row 8: K4, (k2tog) 6 times, k10 (20 sts).

Row 9: P9, (p2tog) 4 times, p3 (16 sts).

Rows 10 and 11: Change to B and k 1 row then p 1 row.

Row 12: K1, (m1, k2) to last st, m1, k1 (24 sts).

Rows 13 to 17: Beg with a p row, work 5 rows in st-st.

Rows 18 and 19: Cast off 3 sts at beg of next 2 rows (18 sts).

Break yarn and set aside.

Left leg

Using the long tail method and A for boot, cast on 18 sts.

Place a marker on cast-on edge between the 11th and 12th st of the sts just cast on.

Row 1 (WS): Purl.

Row 2: K2, (m1, k2) to end (26 sts).

Rows 3 to 7: Beg with a p row, work 5 rows in st-st.

Row 8: K10, (k2tog) 6 times, k4 (20 sts).

Row 9: P3, (p2tog) 4 times, p9 (16 sts).

Rows 10 and 11: Change to B and k 1 row then p 1 row.

Row 12: K1, (m1, k2) to last st, m1, k1 (24 sts).

Rows 13 to 17: Beg with a p row, work 5 rows in st-st.

Rows 18 and 19: Cast off 3 sts at beg of next 2 rows (18 sts).

Join legs

Row 20: K across sts of left leg then with the same yarn cont k across sts of right leg (36 sts).

Rows 21 to 23: Beg with a p row, work 3 rows in st-st.

Row 24: K2, (k2tog, k4) to last 4 sts, k2tog, k2 (30 sts).

Place a marker on last row for waist gathering.

Rows 25 to 34: Beg with a p row, work 10 rows in st-st, ending with a RS row.

Row 35: P5, (p2tog) 3 times, p8, (p2tog) 3 times, p5 (24 sts).

Rows 36 and 37: Change to C for head and work 2 rows in st-st.

Row 38: K2, (m1, k4) to last 2 sts, m1, k2 (30 sts).

Rows 39 to 47: Beg with a p row, work 9 rows in st-st.

Row 48: (K2tog, k1) to end (20 sts).

Row 49: Purl.

Row 50: (K2tog) to end (10 sts).

Thread yarn through sts on needle and leave loose.

SKIRT OF JACKET AND BELT

Using the long tail method and D, cast on 45 sts, WS facing to beg.

Rows 1 to 3: Beg with a p row, work 3 rows in st-st (this part is turned under).

Rows 4 to 9: Work 6 rows in g-st.

Rows 10 to 15: Change to B and beg with a k row, work 6 rows in st-st.

Change to A for belt and dec:

Row 16: (K2tog, k3) to end (36 sts).

Rows 17 and 18: K 1 row then p 1 row. Cast off kwise.

BOOT TOPS (make 2)

Using the long tail method and D, cast on 24 sts.

Row 1 (RS): Knit.

Cast off kwise.

SLEEVES AND HANDS (make 2)

Beg at shoulder using the long tail method and B, cast on 5 sts.

Row 1 (WS): Purl.

Row 2: K1, (m1, k1) to end (9 sts).

Row 3: Purl.

Row 4: K1, m1, k to last st, m1, k1 (11 sts).

Rows 5 and 6: Rep rows 3 and 4 once (13 sts).

Rows 7 to 11: Beg with a p row, work 5 rows in st-st.

Change to C for hand and dec:

Row 12: K3, (k2tog, k3) twice (11 sts).

Rows 13 to 17: Beg with a p row, work 5 rows in st-st.

Row 18: K2tog, (k1, k2tog) to end (7 sts).

Thread yarn through sts on needle, pull tight and secure by threading yarn a second time through sts.

CUFFS (make 2)

Using the long tail method and D, cast on 15 sts, RS facing to beg.

Row 1 (RS): Knit.

Cast off kwise.

NOSE

Using the long tail method and B, cast on 6 sts.

Thread yarn through sts on needle, pull tight and secure by threading yarn a second time through sts.

HAT

Using the long tail method and D, cast on 32 sts and beg in g-st, RS facing to beg.

Rows 1 to 4: Work 4 rows in g-st.

Rows 5 to 10: Change to B and beg with a k row, work 6 rows in st-st.

Row 11: K2tog, k to last 2 sts, k2tog (30 sts).

Row 12: Purl.

Rows 13 to 16: Rep rows 11 and 12 twice more (26 sts).

Row 17: K2tog, (k4, k2tog) to end (21 sts).

Row 18: Purl.

Row 19: (K2tog) twice, k to last 4 sts, (k2tog) twice (17 sts).

Rows 20 to 24: Beg with p row, work 5 rows in st-st.

Row 25: K2tog, k to last 2 sts, k2tog (15 sts).

Row 26: Purl.

Rows 27 to 36: Rep rows 25 and 26, 5 times more (5 sts).

Work bobble

Row 37: Change to D and k 1 row. Cont in rev st-st and inc:

Row 38: K1, (m1, k1) to end (9 sts).

Row 39: Pfb, (p1, pfb) to end (14 sts).

Rows 40 to 43: Beg with a k row, work 4 rows in rev st-st.

Row 44: (K2tog) to end (7 sts).

Thread yarn through sts on needle, pull tight and secure by threading yarn a second time through sts.

BEARD (make 2 pieces)

Using the long tail method and D, cast on 2 sts and work in g-st.

Row 1 (RS): (Kfb) twice (4 sts).

Row 2: Knit.

Row 3: Kfb, k to last st, kfb (6 sts).

Row 4: Knit.

Rows 5 to 10: Rep rows 3 and 4, 3 times more (12 sts).

Row 11: (Kfb) twice, k to last 2 sts, (kfb) twice (16 sts).

Row 12: Knit.

Rows 13 to 16: Rep rows 11 and 12 twice more (24 sts).

Row 17: K2tog, k to last 2 sts, k2tog (22 sts).

Row 18: Knit.

Row 19: (K2tog) 5 times, k2, (k2tog) 5 times (12 sts).

Cast off.

MOUSTACHE
Using the long tail method and D, cast on 6 sts, RS facing to beg. Cast off pwise.

MAKING UP
Note: Sew up all row-end seams on right side using mattress stitch one stitch in from the edge, unless otherwise stated; a one-stitch seam allowance has been allowed for this.

Boots, legs, body and head
Sew up row ends of boots. With markers at tips of toes, oversew cast-on stitches; leg seam will be ½in (12mm) on inside edge of heel. Place a ball of stuffing into toes. Sew up row ends of legs and sew round crotch. Stuff legs, sew up row ends of body and head, and stuff body and head. Pull stitches on a thread tight at top of head and fasten off. To shape neck, take a double piece of yarn to match body and sew a running stitch round last row of body at neck, sewing in and out of every half stitch. Pull tight and knot yarn and sew ends into neck. To shape waist, take a double piece of red yarn and sew a running stitch round row with marker at waist. Pull waist in, knot yarn and sew ends into waist.

Boot tops
Place boot tops around top of boots and oversew row ends. Sew boot tops to doll all the way round.

Skirt of jacket and belt
Turn under lower edge and hem in place. Sew up row ends of skirt of jacket and belt and place on doll. Sew belt to body all the way round.

Sleeves, hands and cuffs
Sew up straight row ends of arms from fingers to underarm and stuff arms using tweezers or tip of scissors. Place cuffs around wrists and oversew row ends. Sew cuffs to wrists all the way round. Leaving armholes open, sew arms to body, sewing top of arms to second row below neck at each side.

Features and buckle
Mark position of eyes with two pins on 6th row above neck, spacing two knitted stitches apart. Embroider eyes in black (see page 218 for how to begin and fasten off the embroidery invisibly), making a small chain stitch beginning at marked position and ending on row above, and work a second chain stitch on top of first. Shade cheeks with a red pencil. Embroider buckle in gold, making four straight double stitches.

Nose
Sew together row ends of nose and sew nose to row below eyes at centre front.

Hat
Sew up row ends of bobble and stuff bobble using tweezers or tip of scissors. Sew up row ends of hat and lightly stuff narrow part of hat. Sew hat to head and fold bobble over and sew to side.

Beard and moustache
Place two pieces of beard together, matching all edges, and oversew row ends. Lightly stuff lower half of beard and oversew cast-off stitches. Sew beard to face, sewing ends of beard to hat, and cast-off edge to face below nose. Shape moustache by winding white yarn tightly around middle and knot at back. Sew moustache below nose.

How to make Mrs Claus

SLIPPERS, LEGS, BODY AND HEAD

Right leg
Using the long tail method and B for slipper, cast on 14 sts.
Place a marker on cast-on edge between the 5th and 6th st of the sts just cast on.
Row 1 (WS): Purl.
Row 2: K2, (m1, k2) to end (20 sts).
Rows 3 to 5: Beg with a p row, work 3 rows in st-st.
Change to C for leg and dec:
Row 6: K2, (k2tog) 6 times, k6 (14 sts).

Row 7: P7, p2tog, p1, p2tog, p2 (12 sts).
Rows 8 to 21: Work 14 rows in st-st.
Break yarn and set aside.

Left leg
Using the long tail method and B for slipper, cast on 14 sts.
Place a marker on cast-on edge between the 9th and 10th st of the sts just cast on.
Row 1 (WS): Purl.
Row 2: K2, (m1, k2) to end (20 sts).
Rows 3 to 5: Beg with a p row, work 3 rows in st-st.

Change to C for leg and dec:
Row 6: K6, (k2tog) 6 times, k2 (14 sts).
Row 7: P2, p2tog, p1, p2tog, p7 (12 sts).
Rows 8 to 21: Work 14 rows in st-st.

Join legs
Row 22: Change to D for lower body and with RS facing, k across sts of left leg then with the same yarn cont k across sts of right leg (24 sts).
Rows 23 to 27: Beg with a p row, work 5 rows in st-st.
Rows 28 to 37: Change to B for upper body and work 10 rows in st-st.

Rows 38 and 39: Change to C for head and work 2 rows in st-st.
Row 40: K2, (m1, k4) to last 2 sts, m1, k2 (30 sts).
Rows 41 to 49: Beg with a p row, work 9 rows in st-st.
Row 50: (K2tog, k1) to end (20 sts).
Row 51: Purl.
Row 52: (K2tog) to end (10 sts).
Thread yarn through sts on needle and leave loose.

SKIRT
Using the long tail method and D, cast on 40 sts, WS facing to beg.
Rows 1 and 2: P 1 row then k 1 row (this part is turned under).
Row 3 (picot edge): P1, k1, (yrn, k2tog) to end.

Rows 4 and 5: K 1 row then p 1 row.
Rows 6 and 7: Change to B and work 2 rows in g-st.
Rows 8 to 23: Beg with a k row, work 16 rows in st-st.
Row 24: (K2tog, k3) to end (32 sts).
Row 25: Purl.
Change to D for waistband and dec:
Row 26: (K2tog, k2) to end (24 sts).
Cast off kwise.

SLEEVES, HANDS AND CUFFS
Make sleeves, hands and cuffs using B for sleeves, C for hands and B for cuffs, as for Cowboy on page 18.

COLLAR
Beg at lower edge using the long tail method and D, cast on 26 sts and work in g-st, RS facing to beg.
Row 1: K6, turn.
Row 2: S1k, k to end.
Row 3: K4, turn.
Row 4: S1k, k to end.
Row 5: K across all sts.
Rows 6 to 9: Rep rows 1 to 4 once.
Cast off in g-st.

HAIR AND BUN
Make hair in D, as for Valentine on page 22 and make bun in D, as for Ballerina on page 34.

APRON AND BOW

Using the long tail method and D, cast on 4 sts.
Row 1 (WS): Purl.
Row 2: K1, m1, k2, m1, k1 (6 sts).
Rows 3 to 9: Beg with a p row, work 7 rows in st-st.
Row 10: K2tog, k2, k2tog (4 sts).
Row 11: Purl.
Cast off.

Frill

Using the long tail method and D, cast on 22 sts, WS facing to beg.
Rows 1 and 2: P 1 row then k 1 row.
Row 3 (picot edge): P1, k1, (yrn, k2tog) to end.
Rows 4 and 5: K 1 row then p 1 row.
Cast off.

Bow

Using the long tail method and D, cast on 30 sts.
Cast off kwise.

MAKING UP

Note: Sew up all row-end seams on right side using mattress stitch one stitch in from the edge, unless otherwise stated; a one-stitch seam allowance has been allowed for this.

Slippers, legs, body and head

Sew up row ends of slippers and ankles. With markers at tips of toes, oversew cast-on stitches; leg seam will be ¼in (6mm) on inside edge of heel. Place a ball of stuffing into toes. Sew up row ends of legs and sew round crotch. Stuff legs, sew up row ends of body and head, and stuff body and head. Pull stitches on a thread tight at top of head and fasten off. To shape neck, take a double length of yarn to match body and sew a running stitch round last row of body at neck, sewing in and out of every half stitch. Pull tight and knot yarn and sew ends into neck. To shape waist, take a double length of red yarn and sew a running stitch round first row of upper body. Pull waist in, knot yarn and sew ends into waist.

Skirt

Fold under lower edge of skirt and hem in place. Sew up row ends of skirt and place skirt on doll. Sew cast-off stitches of waistband to waist of doll all the way round.

Sleeves, hands and cuffs

Make up sleeves, hands and cuffs, as for Cowboy on page 19.

Features, hair, bun and hair bow

Work features, as for Skateboarder on page 15. Make up hair, as for Valentine on page 22. Make up bun, as for Ballerina on page 35. Make a twisted cord (see page 218) for hair bow out of one strand of red yarn, beginning with the yarn 24in (60cm) long. Tie twisted cord into a small bow. Sew bow to hair, sewing through knot of bow to secure and knot and trim ends to ⅓in (8mm).

Collar

Place collar around neck and join at front under chin. Sew collar to neck all the way round and sew points of collar to chest.

Apron and bow

Fold frill along picot edge and oversew cast-on and cast-off stitches. Sew frill around apron and sew apron to waist at front of doll. Shape bow into a bow shape and sew together then sew bow to back of waistband of skirt.

Buttons

Embroider buttons in green, making three horizontal stitches down front of body.

Pilgrims

Materials

♥ Any DK (US: light worsted) yarn
(amounts given are approximate):
10g black (A)
10g white (B)
10g dark grey (C)
10g pale pink (D)
5g brown (E)
10g silver grey (F)
♥ Oddments of black, red, mustard and silver
grey for embroidery and silver grey and
white for making up
♥ 1 pair of 3.25mm (UK10:US3) needles
and a spare needle of the same size
♥ Knitters' pins and a blunt-ended needle
for sewing up
♥ Tweezers (optional)
♥ Acrylic toy stuffing
♥ A red pencil for shading cheeks

Finished size

Boy Pilgrim stands 7in (18cm) tall
Girl Pilgrim stands 6in (15cm) tall

Tension

26 sts x 34 rows measure 4in (10cm)
square over st-st using 3.25mm needles
and DK yarn before stuffing

Abbreviations

See page 219

How to make Boy Pilgrim

SHOES, LEGS, BODY AND HEAD
Right leg

Using the long tail method and A for shoe, cast on 14 sts.

Place a marker on cast-on edge between the 5th and 6th st of the sts just cast on.

Row 1 (WS): Purl.

Row 2: K2, (m1, k2) to end (20 sts).

Rows 3 to 5: Beg with a p row, work 3 rows in st-st.

Row 6: K2, (k2tog) 6 times, k6 (14 sts). Change to B for leg and dec:

Row 7: P7, p2tog, p1, p2tog, p2 (12 sts).

Rows 8 to 21: Work 14 rows in st-st. Break yarn and set aside.

Left leg

Using the long tail method and A for shoe, cast on 14 sts.

Place a marker on cast-on edge between the 9th and 10th st of the sts just cast on.

Row 1 (WS): Purl.

Row 2: K2, (m1, k2) to end (20 sts).

Rows 3 to 5: Beg with a p row, work 3 rows in st-st.

Row 6: K6, (k2tog) 6 times, k2 (14 sts). Change to B for leg and dec:

Row 7: P2, p2tog, p1, p2tog, p7 (12 sts).

Rows 8 to 21: Work 14 rows in st-st.

Join legs

Row 22: With RS facing, k across sts of left leg then with the same yarn cont k across sts of right leg (24 sts). Place a marker on first and last st of last row.

Rows 23 to 25: Beg with a p row, work 3 rows in st-st.

Rows 26 to 37: Change to C for upper body and work 12 rows in st-st.

Rows 38 and 39: Change to D for head and work 2 rows in st-st.

Row 40: K2, (m1, k4) to last 2 sts, m1, k2 (30 sts).

Rows 41 to 49: Beg with a p row, work 9 rows in st-st.

Row 50: (K2tog, k1) to end (20 sts).

Row 51: Purl.

Row 52: (K2tog) to end (10 sts). Thread yarn through sts on needle and leave loose.

BREECHES
First leg

Beg at lower edge using the long tail method and C, cast on 21 sts, RS facing to beg.

Rows 1 to 6: Beg with a k row, work 6 rows in st-st.

Rows 7 and 8: Cast off 2 sts at beg of next 2 rows (17 sts). Break yarn and set aside.

Second leg

Work as for first leg but do not break yarn.

Join legs

Row 9: With RS facing, k across sts of second leg then with the same yarn, cont k across sts of first leg (34 sts).
Rows 10 to 12: Beg with a p row, work 3 rows in st-st.
Cast off.

SKIRT OF JACKET AND BELT
First side

Beg at lower edge using the long tail method and C, cast on 22 sts and beg in g-st, RS facing to beg.
Rows 1 and 2: Work 2 rows in g-st.
Rows 3 to 10: Beg with a k row, work 8 rows in st-st and k to first 2 and last 2 sts on every p row.
Break yarn and set aside.

Second side

Work as for first side.

Join skirt of jacket

Change to A for belt and dec:
Row 11: With RS facing and A, work on second side of skirt of jacket and k2, (k2tog, k2) 5 times, then with the same yarn continue across first side of skirt of jacket and k2, (k2tog, k2) 5 times (34 sts).
Row 12: Knit.
Cast off pwise.

SLEEVES AND HANDS

Make sleeves and hands using C for sleeves and D for hands, as for Cowboy on page 18.

CUFFS (make 2)

Using the long tail method and B, cast on 12 sts and work in g-st, RS facing to beg.
Rows 1 to 3: Work 3 rows in g-st.
Cast off in g-st.

HAIR

Make hair in E, as for Groom on page 48.

COLLAR

Make collar in B, as for Mrs Claus on page 159.

HAT

Beg at brim using the long tail method and A, cast on 48 sts and beg in g-st, RS facing to beg.
Rows 1 to 4: Work 4 rows in g-st.
Join on F for hat band and dec:
Row 5: (K2tog, k1) to end (32 sts).
Rows 6 to 8: Beg with a p row, work 3 rows in st-st.
Cont in A and dec:
Row 9: (K2tog, k6) to end (28 sts).
Rows 10 to 12: Beg with a p row, work 3 rows in st-st.
Row 13: (K2tog, k5) to end (24 sts).
Row 14: Purl.
Row 15: (K2tog, k4) to end (20 sts).
Row 16: K 1 row to mark top of hat.

Shape top

Row 17: (K2tog, k2) to end (15 sts).
Row 18: Purl.
Row 19: (K2tog, k1) to end (10 sts).
Row 20: (P2tog) to end (5 sts).
Thread yarn through sts on needle, pull tight and secure by threading yarn a second time through sts.

MAKING UP

Note: Sew up all row-end seams on right side using mattress stitch one stitch in from the edge, unless otherwise stated; a one-stitch seam allowance has been allowed for this.

Shoes, legs, body and head

Sew up row ends of shoes and ankles. With markers at tips of toes, oversew cast-on stitches; leg seam will be ¼in (6mm) on inside edge of heel. Place a ball of stuffing into toes and sew up row ends of legs. Bring markers together at crotch and sew round crotch. Stuff legs, sew up row ends of body and head, and stuff body and head. Pull stitches on a thread tight at top of head and fasten off. To shape neck, take a double piece of yarn to match body and sew a running stitch round last row of body at neck, sewing in and out of every half stitch. Pull tight, knot yarn and sew ends into neck.

Breeches

Sew up row ends of legs and sew round crotch. Sew up row ends at centre back and place breeches on doll. Sew cast-off stitches of breeches to first row of upper body all the way round.

Skirt of jacket and belt

Oversew row ends of belt and place skirt of jacket on doll. Sew belt to row above breeches at waist using back stitch all the way round.

Sleeves and hands

Make up sleeves and hands, as for Cowboy on page 19.

Cuffs

Place cuffs around wrists and oversew row ends of cast-off stitches at wrist. Sew lower edge of cuffs to wrists all the way round.

Features and hair

Work features and make up hair, as for Groom on page 51.

Collar

Make up collar, as for Mrs Claus on page 161.

Hat

Sew up row ends of hat and stuff top of hat lightly. Place hat on head and pin and sew hat to head using back stitch between brim and hat band, sewing through hat to head all the way round.

Shoe straps, buckles and buttons

Using picture as a guide, embroider a buckle on belt (see page 218 for how to begin and fasten off the embroidery invisibly). Embroider shoes by sewing four horizontal stitches in black over two stitches on the white sock and a buckle in mustard. Embroider a large buckle at centre front of hat in mustard, using a double stitch. Embroider buttons in silver grey at front of jacket using long stitches.

How to make Girl Pilgrim

BOOTS, LEGS, BODY AND HEAD

Make boots, legs, body and head using A for boots, D for legs, B for lower body, F for upper body and D for head, as for Cowboy on page 17.

PETTICOAT

Beg at lower edge using the long tail method and B, cast on 40 sts.

Row 1 (RS): Knit.

Row 2: K2, (yrn, k2tog) to end.

Rows 3 and 4: Work 2 rows in g-st.

Rows 5 to 18: Beg with a k row, work 14 rows in st-st.

Row 19: (K2tog, k2) to end (30 sts).

Row 20: Purl.

Cast off.

SKIRT

Beg at lower edge using the long tail method and A, cast on 50 sts and beg in g-st, RS facing to beg.

Rows 1 and 2: Work 2 rows in g-st.

Rows 3 to 14: Beg with a k row, work 12 rows in st-st.

Row 15: (K2tog, k3) to end (40 sts).

Rows 16 to 22: Beg with a p row, work 7 rows in st-st.

Row 23: (K2tog, k2) to end (30 sts).

Cast off pwise.

APRON

Beg at lower edge using the long tail method and F, cast on 40 sts and beg in g-st, RS facing to beg.

Rows 1 and 2: Work 2 rows in g-st.

Rows 3 to 18: Beg with a k row, work 16 rows in st-st and k to first 2 and last 2 sts on every p row.

Row 19: K1, (k2tog, k2) to last 3 sts, k2tog, k1 (30 sts).

Cast off pwise.

SLEEVES AND HANDS

Make sleeves and hands using A for sleeves and D for hands, as for Cowboy on page 18.

CUFFS

Make cuffs in B, as for Boy Pilgrim.

HAIR

Make hair in E, as for Valentine on page 22.

COLLAR

Make collar in B, as for Mrs Claus on page 159.

BONNET

Beg at peak using the long tail method and B, cast on 30 sts and beg in g-st.

Row 1 (RS): Knit.

Row 2: K to last 3 sts, turn.

Row 3: S1k, k to last 3 sts, turn.

Row 4: S1k, k18, turn.

Row 5: S1k, k13, turn.

Row 6: S1k, k to end.

Row 7: Knit.

Rows 8 and 9: K 1 row then p 1 row.

Row 10: K12, (m1, k3) 3 times, k9 (33 sts).

Rows 11 to 21: Beg with a p row, work 11 rows in st-st.

Row 22: K8, (k2tog, k1) 6 times, k7 (27 sts).

Rows 23 to 25: Beg with a p row, work 3 rows in st-st.

Row 26: K8, (k2tog, k1) 4 times, k7 (23 sts).

Cast off pwise.

MAKING UP

Note: Sew up all row-end seams on right side using mattress stitch one stitch in from the edge, unless otherwise stated; a one-stitch seam allowance has been allowed for this.

Boots, legs, body and head

Make up boots, legs, body and head, as for Cowboy on page 19.

Petticoat

Sew up row ends of petticoat and with seam at centre back, place on doll. Sew cast-off stitches to last row of lower body all the way round.

Skirt

Sew up row ends of skirt and with seam at centre back, place on doll. Sew cast-off stitches of skirt to first row of upper body all the way round.

Apron

Place apron around doll and sew row ends of cast-off stitches together at centre back. Sew cast-off stitches of apron to doll on row above skirt.

Sleeves and hands

Make up sleeves and hands, as for Cowboy on page 19.

Cuffs

Make up cuffs, as for Boy Pilgrim.

Features and hair

Work features, as for Skateboarder on page 15. Make up hair, as for Valentine on page 23.

Collar

Make up collar, as for Mrs Claus on page 161.

Bonnet

Fold cast-off stitches of bonnet in half and oversew. Place bonnet on head and sew lower edge to top of collar. Sew around face and turn brim back.

Bows

Make two bows, one in white and one in silver grey, making a twisted cord (see page 218) out of one strand of yarn for each bow, beginning with the yarn 24in (60cm) long. Tie each twisted cord into a small bow, and sew white bow to bonnet under chin and silver grey bow to back of apron, sewing through knot to secure. Knot and trim ends to ½in (13mm).

Rugby Player

Materials

♥ Any DK (US: light worsted) yarn
  (amounts given are approximate):
  5g black (A)
  5g red (B)
  5g pale pink (C)
  5g white (D)
  5g dark brown (E)
  2g green (F)
♥ Oddments of black, red and gold for
  embroidery
♥ 1 pair of 3.25mm (UK10:US3) needles
  and a spare needle of the same size
♥ Knitters' pins and a blunt-ended needle
  for sewing up
♥ Tweezers (optional)
♥ Acrylic toy stuffing
♥ A red pencil for shading cheeks

Finished size

Rugby Player stands 6in (15cm) tall

Tension

26 sts x 34 rows measure 4in (10cm)
square over st-st using 3.25mm needles
and DK yarn before stuffing

Abbreviations

See page 219

How to make Rugby Player

BOOTS, SOCKS, LEGS, BODY AND HEAD
Right leg
Using the long tail method and A for boot, cast on 14 sts.

Place a marker on cast-on edge between the 5th and 6th st of the sts just cast on.

Row 1 (WS): Purl.

Row 2: K2, (m1, k2) to end (20 sts).

Rows 3 to 5: Beg with a p row, work 3 rows in st-st.

Row 6: K2, (k2tog) 6 times, k6 (14 sts). Change to B for sock and dec:

Row 7: P7, p2tog, p1, p2tog, p2 (12 sts).

Rows 8 to 11: Work 4 rows in st-st.

Rows 12 to 21: Change to C for leg and work 10 rows in st-st. Break yarn and set aside.

Left leg
Using the long tail method and A for boot, cast on 14 sts.

Place a marker on cast-on edge between the 9th and 10th st of the sts just cast on.

Row 1 (WS): Purl.

Row 2: K2, (m1, k2) to end (20 sts).

Rows 3 to 5: Beg with a p row, work 3 rows in st-st.

Row 6: K6, (k2tog) 6 times, k2 (14 sts). Change to B for sock and dec:

Row 7: P2, p2tog, p1, p2tog, p7 (12 sts).

Rows 8 to 11: Work 4 rows in st-st.

Rows 12 to 21: Change to C for leg and work 10 rows in st-st.

Join legs
Row 22: Change to D for lower body and with RS facing, k across sts of left leg then with the same yarn cont k across sts of right leg (24 sts).

Rows 23 to 27: Beg with a p row, work 5 rows in st-st.

Rows 28 to 37: Change to C for upper body and work 10 rows in st-st. Place a marker on last row for neck gathering.

Rows 38 and 39: Work 2 rows in st-st.

Row 40: K2, (m1, k4) to last 2 sts, m1, k2 (30 sts).

Rows 41 to 49: Beg with a p row, work 9 rows in st-st.

Row 50: (K2tog, k1) to end (20 sts).

Row 51: Purl.

Row 52: (K2tog) to end (10 sts). Thread yarn through sts on needle and leave loose.

SHORTS
Make shorts in D, as for Tennis Player on page 53.

SOCK TOPS
Make sock tops in D, as for Footballer on page 140.

ARMS AND HANDS
Make arms and hands in C, as for Skateboarder on pages 13 and 14.

RUGBY SHIRT

Note: Sleeves are worked first and knitted into body.

Sleeves (make 2)

Using the long tail method and B, cast on 16 sts, RS facing to beg.
Rows 1 to 9: Beg with a k row, work 9 rows in st-st, finishing with a RS row.
Row 10: Cast off 3 sts pwise, p9, cast off rem 3 sts pwise and fasten off (10 sts).
Set aside.
Rep second sleeve as for first sleeve and set aside.

Front and back

Using the long tail method and B, cast on 38 sts, RS facing to beg.
Rows 1 to 7: Beg with a k row, work 7 rows in st-st finishing with a RS row.

Divide for armholes

Row 8: P8, cast off 4 sts pwise, p13, cast off 4 sts pwise, p7 (30 sts).

Join sleeves

Row 9: With RS of all pieces facing, k8 from left back, k10 from one sleeve, k14 across front, k10 from other sleeve, k8 from right back (50 sts).
Row 10: P6, (p2tog) twice, p6, (p2tog) twice, p10, (p2tog) twice, p6, (p2tog) twice, p6 (42 sts).
Row 11: K5, (k2tog) twice, k4, (k2tog) twice, k8, (k2tog) twice, k4, (k2tog) twice, k5 (34 sts).

Divide for front opening

Row 12: P16, cast off 2 sts pwise, p15 (32 sts).

Work left back and left front

Row 13: K4, (k2tog) twice, k2, (k2tog) twice, k2, turn and work on these 12 sts.
Row 14: Purl.

Work collar

Change to D and dec:
Row 15: K3, k2tog, k2, k2tog, k3 (10 sts).
Row 16: Knit.
Row 17: P2, (m1, p2) 3 times, m1, p1, k1 (14 sts).
Row 18: Knit.
Row 19: P to last st, k1.
Row 20: Knit.
Cast off kwise.

Work right front and right back

Row 21: Rejoin B to rem sts and K2, (k2tog) twice, k2, (k2tog) twice, k4 (12 sts).
Row 22: Purl.

Work collar

Change to D and dec:
Row 23: K3, k2tog, k2, k2tog, k3 (10 sts).
Row 24: Knit.
Row 25: K1, p1, (m1, p2) 3 times, m1, p2 (14 sts).
Row 26: Knit.
Row 27: K1, p to end.
Row 28: Knit.
Cast off kwise.

Neck border

Using the thumb method and D, cast on 10 sts.
Cast off pwise.

HAIR

Using the long tail method and E, cast on 21 sts.
Row 1: K1, *k next st but don't slip it off the needle, bring yarn forward

between the needles and wrap around a pencil to make a loop, take yarn back and k the same st again, slipping it off LH needle and pass the first of these sts over the second and off RH needle, k1, rep from * to end.

Row 2: P1, (p2tog) to end (11 sts).

Row 3: As row 1.

Thread yarn through sts on needle, pull tight and secure by threading yarn a second time through sts.

HEADBAND

Using the long tail method and D, cast on 30 sts.
Cast off kwise.

RUGBY BALL

Using the long tail method and D, cast on 6 sts, WS facing to beg.

Row 1 and foll alt row: Purl.

Row 2: K1, (m1, k1) to end (11 sts).

Row 4: K1, (m1, k2) to end (16 sts).

Rows 5 to 7: Beg with a p row, work 3 rows in st-st.

Row 8: K1, (m1, k3) to end (21 sts).

Rows 9 to 11: Beg with a p row, work 3 rows in st-st.

Row 12: K1, (k2tog, k2) to end (16 sts).

Rows 13 to 15: Beg with a p row, work 3 rows in st-st.

Row 16: K1, (k2tog, k1) to end (11 sts).

Row 17: Purl.

Row 18: K1, (k2tog) to end (6 sts).

Thread yarn through sts on needle, pull tight and secure by threading yarn a second time through sts.

Trim

Using the long tail method and F, cast on 8 sts.

Row 1 (RS): Purl.
Cast off kwise.

MAKING UP

Note: Sew up all row-end seams on right side using mattress stitch one stitch in from the edge, unless otherwise stated; a one-stitch seam allowance has been allowed for this.

Boots, legs, body and head

Sew up row ends of boots. With markers at tips of toes, oversew cast-on stitches; leg seam will be ¼in (6mm) on inside edge of heel. Place a ball of stuffing into toes, sew up row ends of socks and legs and sew round crotch. Stuff legs, sew up row ends of body and head, and stuff body and head. Pull stitches on a thread tight at top of head and fasten off. To shape neck, take a double piece of pale pink yarn and sew a running stitch round row with marker at neck, sewing in and out of every half stitch. Pull tight, knot yarn and sew ends into neck.

Shorts

Make up shorts, as for Tennis Player on page 55.

Sock tops

Make up sock tops, as for Footballer on page 141.

Arms and hands

Make up arms and hands, as for Skateboarder on page 15.

Rugby shirt

Sew up sleeve seams of rugby shirt and sew across under arm. Place rugby shirt on doll and sew up back seam. Turn collar down and fold neck border in half then sew neck border to front opening. Sew collar down.

Features and badge

Work features, as for Skateboarder on page 15. Using picture as a guide, embroider badge on rugby shirt in gold.

Hair and headband

Sew up row ends of hair then place on top of head and sew in place. Place head band around hair and sew together at back. Sew headband to head all the way round.

Rugby ball

Gather round cast-on stitches of rugby ball, pull tight and secure. Sew up row ends, leaving a gap, stuff and sew up gap. Sew trim to side of rugby ball and embroider stitches in black.

Fisherman

Materials

- ♥ Any DK (US: light worsted) yarn
  (amounts given are approximate):
  5g green (A)
  5g pale pink (B)
  5g white (C)
  10g gold (D)
  5g brown (E)
  5g beige (F)
  2g silver grey (G)
- ● Oddments of black and red for embroidery
  and beige for making up
- ♥ 1 pair of 3.25mm (UK10:US3) needles and
  a spare needle of the same size
- ♥ Knitters' pins and a blunt-ended needle
  for sewing up
- ♥ Tweezers (optional)
- ♥ Acrylic toy stuffing
- ♥ 1 plastic drinking straw
  (³/₁₆in/5mm diameter)
- ♥ A red pencil for shading cheeks

Finished size

Fisherman stands 6in (15cm) tall

Tension

26 sts x 34 rows measure 4in (10cm)
square over st-st using 3.25mm needles
and DK yarn before stuffing

Abbreviations

See page 219

How to make Fisherman

BOOTS, LEGS, BODY AND HEAD

Make boots, legs, body and head using A for boots, B for legs, C for lower body, D for upper body and B for head, as for Prince on page 131.

TROUSERS
First leg
Beg at lower edge using the long tail method and D, cast on 21 sts, WS facing to beg.
Rows 1 to 7: Beg with a p row, work 7 rows in st-st.
Rows 8 and 9: Cast off 2 sts at beg of next 2 rows (17 sts).
Break yarn and set aside.

Second leg
Work second leg as for first leg but do not break yarn.

Join legs
Row 10: With RS facing, k across sts of second leg then with the same yarn cont k across sts of first leg (34 sts).
Rows 11 to 15: Beg with a p row, work 5 rows in st-st.
Cast off.

BOOT TOPS
Make boot tops in A, as for Prince on page 132.

ARMS, HANDS AND HAIR
Make arms and hands in B and hair in E, as for Skateboarder on pages 13 and 14.

WATERPROOF JACKET
Note: Sleeves are worked first and knitted into body.

Sleeves (make 2)
Beg at cuff using the long tail method and D, cast on 16 sts.
Row 1 (RS): Purl.
Rows 2 to 9: Beg with a p row, work 8 rows in st-st, finishing with a RS row.
Row 10: Cast off 3 sts pwise, p9, cast off rem 3 sts pwise and fasten off (10 sts).
Set aside.
Rep second sleeve as for first sleeve and set aside.

Front and back
Using the long tail method and D, cast on 42 sts.
Row 1 (RS): Purl.
Rows 2 to 11: Beg with a p row, work 10 rows in st-st and k the first 2 and last 2 sts on every p row, ending with a RS row.

Divide for armholes
Row 12: K2, p8, cast off 4 sts pwise, p13, cast off 4 sts pwise, p7, k2 (34 sts).

Join sleeves
Row 13: With RS of all pieces facing, k10 from right front, k10 from one sleeve, k14 across back, k10 from other sleeve, k10 from left front (54 sts).
Row 14: K2, p6, (p2tog) twice, p6, (p2tog) twice, p10, (p2tog) twice, p6, (p2tog) twice, p6, k2 (46 sts).
Row 15: K7, (k2tog) twice, k4, (k2tog) twice, k8, (k2tog) twice, k4, (k2tog) twice, k7 (38 sts).
Row 16: K2, p to last 2 sts, k2.
Row 17: K6, (k2tog) twice, k2, (k2tog) twice, k6, (k2tog) twice, k2, (k2tog) twice, k6 (30 sts).
Row 18: As row 16.

Work collar
Rows 19 and 20: Work 2 rows in g-st.
Row 21: K2, m1, k to last 2 sts, m1, k2 (32 sts).
Rows 22 to 24: Work 3 rows in g-st. Cast off in g-st.

SOU'WESTER
Using the long tail method and D, cast on 48 sts and beg in g-st, RS facing to beg.
Rows 1 to 5: Work 5 rows in g-st.
Row 6: (K2tog, k2) to end (36 sts).
Rows 7 to 15: Beg with a p row, work 9 rows in st-st.
Row 16: (K2tog, k1) to end (24 sts).
Row 17 and foll alt row: Purl.
Row 18: (K2tog, k1) to end (16 sts).
Row 20: (K2tog) to end (8 sts).
Thread yarn through sts on needle, pull tight and secure by threading yarn a second time through sts.

FISHING ROD AND FISH
Rod
Using the long tail method and F, cast on 6 sts and work in rev st-st, RS facing to beg.
Beg with a p row, work in rev st-st for 5½in (14cm).
Cast off.

Reel (make 2 pieces)
Using the long tail method and F, cast on 12 sts.
Row 1 (RS): (K2tog) to end (6 sts).
Thread yarn through sts on needle, pull tight and secure by threading yarn a second time through sts.

Fish
Beg at tail and using the long tail method and G, cast on 12 sts.
Row 1 (WS): Purl.
Row 2: (K2tog) to end (6 sts).
Row 3: Purl.
Row 4: K1, (m1, k1) to end (11 sts).
Rows 5 to 9: Beg with a p row, work 5 rows in st-st.
Row 10: K2tog, (k1, k2tog) to end (7 sts).
Row 11: Purl.

Thread yarn through sts on needle, pull tight and secure by threading yarn a second time through sts.

MAKING UP
Note: Sew up all row-end seams on right side using mattress stitch one stitch in from the edge, unless otherwise stated; a one-stitch seam allowance has been allowed for this.

Boots, legs, body and head
Make up boots, legs, body and head, as for Cowboy on page 19.

Trousers
Sew up leg seams of trousers and sew round crotch. Sew up row ends at centre back and place trousers on doll. Sew cast-off stitches of trousers to first row of upper body all the way round, and sew cast-on stitches of each leg to last row of boot.

Boot tops
Make up boot tops, as for Prince on page 133.

Arms, hands, features and hair
Make up arms and hands, work features and make up hair, as for Skateboarder on page 15.

Waterproof jacket and buttons
Sew up sleeve seams of jacket and sew across underarm. Place jacket on doll and sew up centre front of jacket. Using picture as a guide, embroider buttons in black down front of jacket, making two small stitches close together for each button.

Sou'wester
Sew up row ends of sou'wester and place on head. Sew sou'wester to head at base of brim, sewing through hat to head. Turn brim up at front.

Fishing rod and fish

Cut a piece of plastic drinking straw to 5in (12.5cm) and place rod around drinking straw. Oversew row ends of rod along length, enclosing drinking straw inside. Gather round top and bottom and pull tight and secure. Make fishing line in beige by making a twisted cord (see page 218) out of one strand of yarn, beginning with the yarn 35in (90cm) long. Tie a knot 7in (18cm) from folded end and trim ends. Place two pieces of reel together and secure knot of line between the two then oversew outer edge. Sew reel to rod 1in (2.5cm) from lower end. Sew line to rod and to tip of rod. Sew up row ends of fish and gather round base of tail, pull tight and secure. Sew mouth of fish to line.

177

Soldier

Materials

- Any DK (US: light worsted) yarn (amounts given are approximate):
  5g black (A)
  5g pale pink (B)
  5g white (C)
  5g red (D)
  5g medium blue (E)
  5g brown (F)
  2g gold (G)
- Oddments of black, red, white and gold for embroidery
- 1 pair of 3.25mm (UK10:US3) needles and a spare needle of the same size
- Knitters' pins and a blunt-ended needle for sewing up
- Tweezers (optional)
- Acrylic toy stuffing
- A red pencil for shading cheeks

Finished size

Soldier stands 7$\frac{1}{2}$in (19cm) tall

Tension

26 sts x 34 rows measure 4in (10cm) square over st-st using 3.25mm needles and DK yarn before stuffing

Abbreviations

See page 219

How to make Soldier

BOOTS, LEGS, BODY AND HEAD
Right leg
Using the long tail method and A for boot, cast on 14 sts.

Place a marker on cast-on edge between the 5th and 6th st of the sts just cast on.

Row 1 (WS): Purl.

Row 2: K2, (m1, k2) to end (20 sts).

Rows 3 to 5: Beg with a p row, work 3 rows in st-st.

Row 6: K2, (k2tog) 6 times, k6 (14 sts).

Row 7: P7, p2tog, p1, p2tog, p2 (12 sts).

Rows 8 and 9: K 1 row then p 1 row.

Rows 10 to 21: Change to B for leg and work 12 rows in st-st.

Break yarn and set aside.

Left leg
Using the long tail method and A for boot, cast on 14 sts.

Place a marker on cast-on edge between the 9th and 10th st of the sts just cast on.

Row 1 (WS): Purl.

Row 2: K2, (m1, k2) to end (20 sts).

Rows 3 to 5: Beg with a p row, work 3 rows in st-st.

Row 6: K6, (k2tog) 6 times, k2 (14 sts).

Row 7: P2, p2tog, p1, p2tog, p7 (12 sts).

Rows 8 and 9: K 1 row then p 1 row.

Rows 10 to 21: Change to B for leg and work 12 rows in st-st.

Join legs
Row 22: Change to C and with RS facing, k across sts of left leg then with the same yarn cont k across sts of right leg (24 sts).

Rows 23 to 25: Beg with a p row, work 3 rows in st-st.

Rows 26 to 37: Change to D for upper body and work 12 rows in st-st.

Rows 38 and 39: Change to B for head and work 2 rows in st-st.

Row 40: K2, (m1, k4) to last 2 sts, m1, k2 (30 sts).

Rows 41 to 49: Beg with a p row, work 9 rows in st-st.

Row 50: (K2tog, k1) to end (20 sts).

Row 51: Purl.

Row 52: (K2tog) to end (10 sts).

Thread yarn through sts on needle and leave loose.

TROUSERS
First leg
Beg at lower edge using the long tail method and E, cast on 21 sts.

Row 1 (RS): Purl.

Rows 2 to 12: Beg with a p row, work 11 rows in st-st.

Rows 13 and 14: Cast off 2 sts at beg of next 2 rows (17 sts).

Break yarn and set aside.

Second leg
Work second leg as for first leg but do not break yarn.

Join legs
Row 15: With RS facing, k across sts of second leg then with the same yarn cont k across sts of first leg (34 sts).
Rows 16 to 18: Beg with a p row, work 3 rows in st-st.
Cast off.

SKIRT OF JACKET AND BELT
Beg at lower edge using the long tail method and C, cast on 40 sts and beg in g-st, RS facing to beg.
Rows 1 and 2: Work 2 rows in g-st.
Rows 3 to 6: Change to D and beg with a k row, work 4 rows in st-st. Change to C for belt and dec:
Row 7: (K2tog, k2) to end (30 sts).
Cast off kwise.

SLEEVES, HANDS AND CUFFS
Make sleeves, hands and cuffs using D for sleeves, B for hands and D for cuffs, as for Cowboy on page 18.

HAIR
Make hair in F, as for Skateboarder on page 14.

MAKING UP

Note: Sew up all row-end seams on right side using mattress stitch one stitch in from the edge, unless otherwise stated; a one-stitch seam allowance has been allowed for this.

Boots, legs, body and head
Make up boots, legs, body and head, as for Cowboy on page 19.

Trousers
Make up trousers, as for Skateboarder on page 15.

Skirt of jacket and belt
Sew up row ends of skirt of jacket and belt and place on doll. Sew belt to doll all the way round.

Sleeves, hands and cuffs
Make up sleeves, hands and cuffs, as for Cowboy on page 19.

Features and hair
Work features and make up hair, as for Skateboarder on page 15.

Bearskin
Sew up row ends and stuff top of bearskin. Pin and sew lower edge of bearskin to head. Sew strap from one side of bearskin, beneath chin and up to other side of bearskin.

BEARSKIN
Using the long tail method and A, cast on 32 sts and work in g-st, RS facing to beg.
Rows 1 to 4: Work 4 rows in g-st.
Row 5: K8, m1, k16, m1, k8 (34 sts).
Rows 6 to 8: Work 3 rows in g-st.
Row 9: K9, m1, k16, m1, k9 (36 sts).
Rows 10 to 12: Work 3 rows in g-st.
Row 13: K9, m1, k18, m1, k9 (38 sts).
Rows 14 to 16: Work 3 rows in g-st.
Row 17: K10, m1, k18, m1, k10 (40 sts).

Rows 18 to 20: Work 3 rows in st-st.
Row 21: (K2tog, k2) to end (30 sts).
Row 22: Knit.
Row 23: (K2tog, k1) to end (20 sts).
Row 24: Knit.
Row 25: (K2tog) to end (10 sts).
Thread yarn through sts on needle, pull tight and secure by threading yarn a second time through sts.

Strap
Using the long tail method and G, cast on 26 sts.
Cast off kwise.

Snowman

Materials

- Any DK (US: light worsted) yarn
  (amounts given are approximate):
  20g white (A)
  5g silver grey (B)
  2g orange (C)
  5g medium blue (D)
  5g pale blue (E)
- Oddment of black for embroidery
- 1 pair of 3.25mm (UK10:US3) needles and
  a spare needle of the same size and a 4mm
  (UK8:US10) needle for scarf only
- Knitters' pins and a blunt-ended needle
  for sewing up
- Tweezers (optional)
- Acrylic toy stuffing

Finished size

Snowman stands 7¹/₂in (19cm) tall

Tension

26 sts x 34 rows measure 4in (10cm)
square over st-st using 3.25mm needles
and DK yarn before stuffing

Abbreviations

See page 219

How to make Snowman

LEGS, BODY AND HEAD
Right leg
Using the long tail method and A for foot, cast on 18 sts.
Place a marker on cast-on edge between the 7th and 8th st of the sts just cast on.
Row 1 (WS): Purl.
Row 2: K2, (m1, k2) to end (26 sts).
Rows 3 to 7: Beg with a p row, work 5 rows in st-st.
Row 8: K4, (k2tog) 6 times, k10 (20 sts).
Row 9: P9, (p2tog) 4 times, p3 (16 sts).
Rows 10 to 17: Work 8 rows in st-st.
Break yarn and set aside.

Left leg
Using the long tail method and A for foot, cast on 18 sts.
Place a marker on cast-on edge between the 11th and 12th st of the sts just cast on.
Row 1 (WS): Purl.
Row 2: K2, (m1, k2) to end (26 sts).
Rows 3 to 7: Beg with a p row, work 5 rows in st-st.
Row 8: K10, (k2tog) 6 times, k4 (20 sts).
Row 9: P3, (p2tog) 4 times, p9 (16 sts).
Rows 10 to 17: Work 8 rows in st-st.

Join legs
Row 18: With RS facing, k across sts of left leg then with the same yarn cont k across sts of right leg (32 sts).
Place a marker on first and last st of last row.
Rows 19 to 37: Beg with a p row, work 19 rows in st-st.
Place a marker on last row for neck gathering.
Rows 38 to 49: Work 12 rows in st-st.
Row 50: (K2tog, k2) to end (24 sts).
Row 51 and foll alt row: Purl.
Row 52: (K2tog, k1) to end (16 sts).
Row 54: (K2tog) to end (8 sts).
Thread yarn through sts on needle and leave loose.

ARMS
Using the long tail method and A, cast on 5 sts.
Row 1 (WS): Purl.
Row 2: K1, (m1, k1) to end (9 sts).
Row 3: Purl.
Row 4: K1, m1, k to last st, m1, k1 (11 sts).

Rows 5 to 8: Rep rows 3 and 4 twice more (15 sts).
Rows 9 to 17: Beg with a p row, work 9 rows in st-st.
Row 18: (K2tog, k1) to end (10 sts).
Thread yarn through sts on needle, pull tight and secure by threading yarn a second time through sts.

WAISTCOAT

Using the long tail method and B, cast on 38 sts and work in g-st.
Row 1 (RS): Knit.
Row 2: K1, m1, k to last st, m1, k1 (40 sts).
Rows 3 and 4: Rep rows 1 and 2 once (42 sts).
Rows 5 to 7: Work 3 rows in g-st, ending with a RS row.

Divide for armholes
Row 8: K8, cast off 4 sts kwise, k17, cast off 4 sts kwise, k7 (34 sts).

Work right front
Row 9: K6, k2tog, turn and work on these 7 sts.
Row 10: Knit.
Row 11: K5, k2tog (6 sts).
Rows 12 to 20: Work 9 rows in g-st.
Row 21: K2tog, k to end (5 sts).
Row 22: Knit.
Rows 23 to 25: Rep rows 21 and 22 once, then row 21 once (3 sts).
Cast off in g-st.

Back
Rejoin yarn to rem sts and dec:
Row 26: K2tog, k14, k2tog, turn and work on these 16 sts.
Row 27: Knit.
Row 28: K2tog, k to last 2 sts, k2tog (14 sts).
Rows 29 to 36: Work 8 rows in g-st ending with a RS row.
Cast off in g-st.

Left front
Rejoin yarn to rem sts and dec:
Row 37: K2tog, k to end (7 sts).
Row 38: Knit.
Row 39: As row 37 (6 sts).
Rows 40 to 48: Work 9 rows in g-st.
Row 49: K to last 2 sts, k2tog (5 sts).
Row 50: Knit.
Rows 51 to 53: Rep row 49 and 50 once then row 49 once (3 sts).
Cast off in g-st.

CARROT NOSE

Using the long tail method and C, cast on 7 sts.
Row 1 (WS): Purl.
Row 2: K1, (k2tog, k1) twice (5 sts).
Row 3: Purl.
Thread yarn through sts on needle, pull tight and secure by threading yarn a second time through sts.

BOBBLE HAT

Beg at lower edge using the long tail method and D, cast on 32 sts and beg in rib, WS of brim facing to beg.
Row 1: (K1, p1) to end.
Rows 2 to 8: Rep row 1, 7 times more.

Rows 9 to 14: Beg with a k row, work 6 rows in st-st.
Row 15: (K2tog, k2) to end (24 sts).
Row 16 and foll alt row: Purl.
Row 17: (K2tog, k1) to end (16 sts).
Row 19: (K2tog) to end (8 sts).
Cont in rev st-st and inc:
Row 20: K1, (m1, k2) to last st, m1, k1 (12 sts).
Rows 21 to 24: Beg with a p row, work 4 rows in rev st-st.
Row 25: (P2tog) to end (6 sts).
Thread yarn through sts on needle, pull tight and secure by threading yarn a second time through sts.

SCARF

Using the long tail method and E, cast on 50 sts and work in g-st, RS facing to beg.

Rows 1 to 5: Work 5 rows in g-st. Cast off using 4mm needle in g-st.

MAKING UP

Note: Sew up all row-end seams on right side using mattress stitch one stitch in from the edge, unless otherwise stated; a one-stitch seam allowance has been allowed for this.

Legs, body and head

Sew up row ends of ankles and with markers at tips of toes, oversew cast-on stitches; leg seam will be ½in (13mm) on inside edge of heel. Place a ball of stuffing into toes. Sew up row ends of legs, bring markers together at crotch and sew round crotch. Stuff legs, sew up row ends of body and head, and stuff body and head. Pull stitches on a thread tight at top of head and fasten off.

To shape neck, take a double piece of white yarn and sew a running stitch round row with marker at neck, sewing in and out of every half stitch. Pull tight, knot yarn and sew ends into neck.

Arms

Sew up straight row ends of arms from fingers to underarm and stuff arms. Leaving armholes open, sew arms to body, sewing top of arms to second row below neck at each side.

Waistcoat

Sew up shoulders and place waistcoat on Snowman.

Carrot nose, features and buttons

Sew up row ends of carrot nose and stuff using tweezers or tip of scissors. Sew nose to face on 6th and 7th rows above neck. Embroider eyes in black (see page 218 for how to begin and fasten off the embroidery invisibly), making a chain stitch for each eye and a second chain stitch on top of first. Make a shallow 'V' in black for mouth below nose. Embroider two buttons, making three straight stitches close together for each button.

Bobble hat

Sew up row ends of bobble and stuff bobble. To shape bobble, use a double length of yarn to match hat and sew a running stitch around base of bobble on inside edge. Pull tight and knot yarn. Sew up row ends of hat, reversing seam for turn up, and place on head and turn up lower edge. Sew hat to head.

Scarf

Tie scarf around neck and sew in place. Make a fringe at both ends of scarf and trim fringe to ½in (13mm).

Builder

Materials

- ♥ Any DK (US: light worsted) yarn
  (amounts given are approximate):
  5g black (A)
  5g pale pink (B)
  5g white (C)
  5g denim blue (D)
  5g mustard (E)
  5g brown (F)
  5g gold (G)
  2g grey (H)
- ♥ Oddments of black, red, white and mustard
  for embroidery
- ♥ 1 pair of 3.25mm (UK10:US3) needles and
  a spare needle of the same size
- ♥ Knitters' pins and a blunt-ended needle
  for sewing up
- ♥ Tweezers (optional)
- ♥ Acrylic toy stuffing
- ♥ A red pencil for shading cheeks

Finished size

Builder stands 6½in (16.5cm) tall

Tension

26 sts x 34 rows measure 4in (10cm)
square over st-st using 3.25mm needles
and DK yarn before stuffing

Abbreviations

See page 219

How to make Builder

BOOTS, LEGS, BODY AND HEAD

Make boots, legs, body and head using A for boots, B for legs, C for lower body, D for upper body and B for head, as for Cowboy on page 17.

SLEEVES, HANDS, ARM CUFFS AND DUNGAREES

Make sleeves, hands, arm cuffs and dungarees using D for sleeves, B for hands, D for arm cuffs, and dungarees in E, as for Painter & Decorator on pages 29 and 30.

HAIR

Make hair in F, as for Skateboarder on page 14.

HARD HAT

Using the long tail method and G, cast on 48 sts and beg in g-st, RS facing to beg.
Rows 1 and 2: Work 2 rows in g-st.
Row 3: (K2tog, k2) to end (36 sts).
Rows 4 to 12: Beg with a p row, work 9 rows in st-st.
Row 13: (K2tog, k1) to end (24 sts).
Row 14 and foll alt row: Purl.
Row 15: (K2tog, k1) to end (16 sts).
Row 17: (K2tog) to end (8 sts).
Thread yarn through sts on needle, pull tight and secure by threading yarn a second time through sts.

TROUSER POCKET

Using the long tail method and E, cast on 6 sts, RS facing to beg.
Rows 1 to 6: Beg with a k row, work 6 rows in st-st.
Cast off.

HAMMER

Using the long tail method and H, cast on 10 sts.
Cast off kwise.

MAKING UP

Note: Sew up all row-end seams on right side using mattress stitch one stitch in from the edge, unless otherwise stated; a one-stitch seam allowance has been allowed for this.

Boots, legs, body and head

Make up boots, legs, body and head, as for Cowboy on page 19.

Sleeves, hands, arm cuffs and dungarees
Make up sleeves, hands, arm cuffs and dungarees, as for Painter & Decorator on page 31.

Features and hair
Work features and make up hair, as for Skateboarder on page 15.

Hard hat
Sew up row ends of hard hat and stuff top of hat. Place on head and sew lower edge of hat to head at base of brim, sewing through hat to head.

Trouser pocket
Sew trouser pocket to right leg of trousers and embroider tool handles in black, red and white.

Hammer
Sew hammer handle to trousers and embroider head of hammer in black and a loop in mustard.

Astronaut

Materials

- Any DK (US: light worsted) yarn
  (amounts given are approximate):
  5g silver grey (A)
  20g white (B)
  5g black (C)
  5g ice blue (D)
  5g petrol blue (E)
- Oddment of black for embroidery
- 1 pair of 3.25mm (UK10:US3) needles
  and a spare needle of the same size
- Knitters' pins and a blunt-ended needle
  for sewing up
- Tweezers (optional)
- Acrylic toy stuffing

Finished size

Astronaut stands 6½in (16.5cm) tall

Tension

26 sts x 34 rows measure 4in (10cm)
square over st-st using 3.25mm needles
and DK yarn before stuffing

Abbreviations

See page 219

How to make Astronaut

BOOTS, LEGS, BODY AND HEAD
Right leg
Using the long tail method and A for boot, cast on 18 sts.
Place a marker on cast-on edge between the 7th and 8th st of the sts just cast on.
Row 1 (WS): Purl.
Row 2: K2, (m1, k2) to end (26 sts).
Row 3: Purl.
Rows 4 to 7: Change to B and work 4 rows in st-st.
Row 8: K4, (k2tog) 6 times, k10 (20 sts).
Row 9: P9, (p2tog) 4 times, p3 (16 sts).
Rows 10 to 15: Work 6 rows in g-st.
Rows 16 to 21: Beg with a k row, work 6 rows in st-st.
Break yarn and set aside.

Left leg
Using the long tail method and A for boot, cast on 18 sts.
Place a marker on cast-on edge between the 11th and 12th st of the sts just cast on.
Row 1 (WS): Purl.
Row 2: K2, (m1, k2) to end (26 sts).
Row 3: Purl.
Rows 4 to 7: Change to B and work 4 rows in st-st.
Row 8: K10, (k2tog) 6 times, k4 (20 sts).
Row 9: P3, (p2tog) 4 times, p9 (16 sts).
Rows 10 to 15: Work 6 rows in g-st.
Rows 16 to 21: Beg with a k row, work 6 rows in st-st.

Join legs
Row 22: With RS facing, k across sts of left leg then with the same yarn cont k across sts of right leg (32 sts). Place a marker on first and last st of last row.
Rows 23 to 35: Beg with a p row, work 13 rows in st-st.

Rows 36 to 39: Join on C and work 4 rows in st-st.
Rows 40 and 41: Cont in B and work 2 rows in st-st.
Row 42: K4, (m1, k8) to last 4 sts, m1, k4 (36 sts).
Rows 43 to 53: Beg with a p row, work 11 rows in st-st.
Row 54: (K2tog, k2) to end (27 sts).
Row 55 and foll alt row: Purl.
Row 56: (K2tog, k1) to end (18 sts).
Row 58: (K2tog) to end (9 sts).
Thread yarn through sts on needle, and leave loose.

ARMS (make 2)
Using the long tail method and B, cast on 5 sts, WS facing to beg.
Row 1 and foll alt row: Purl.
Row 2: K1, (m1, k1) to end (9 sts).
Row 4: K1, m1, k to last st, m1, k1 (11 sts).
Row 5: Purl.
Rows 6 to 9: Rep rows 4 and 5 twice more (15 sts).
Rows 10 to 13: Work 4 rows in st-st.

Rows 14 to 17: Join on D and work 4 rows in g-st.
Rows 18 to 21: Cont in C and beg with a k row, work 4 rows in st-st.
Row 22: (K2tog, k1) to end (10 sts).
Thread yarn through sts on needle, pull tight and secure by threading yarn a second time through sts.

BELT
Using the long tail method and A, cast on 40 sts and work in g-st.
Row 1 (RS): K23, turn.
Row 2: S1k, k5, turn.
Row 3: S1k, k to end.
Row 4: Knit.
Rows 5 to 7: Rep rows 1 to 3 once.
Cast off in g-st, loosely.

SHOULDER STRAPS
(make 2)
Using the long tail method and D, cast on 20 sts.
Row 1 (RS): Knit.
Cast off kwise.

EYE PIECE
Using the long tail method and A, cast on 10 sts, WS facing to beg.
Rows 1 to 3: Beg with a p row, work 3 rows in st-st.
Cast off.

BACKPACK
Using the long tail method and B, cast on 18 sts.
Row 1 (WS): Purl.
Row 2: (K1, m1) twice, k14, (m1, k1) twice (22 sts).
Rows 3 to 19: Beg with a p row, work 17 rows in st-st.
Row 20: (K1, k2tog) twice, k10 (k2tog, k1) twice (18 sts).
Row 21: Purl.
Row 22: Knit.
Rows 23 to 43: Rep rows 1 to 21 once.
Cast off.

AIR TUBE
Using the long tail method and A, cast on 6 sts.
Row 1 (RS): Purl.
Row 2: Change to E and p 1 row.
Rows 3 to 6: K 2 rows then p 2 rows.
Rows 7 to 38: Rep rows 3 to 6, 8 times more.
Cast off.

MAKING UP
Note: Sew up all row-end seams on right side using mattress stitch one stitch in from the edge, unless otherwise stated; a one-stitch seam allowance has been allowed for this.

Boots, legs, body and head

Sew up row ends of boots and with markers at tips of toes, oversew cast-on stitches; leg seam will be $\frac{1}{2}$in (13mm) on inside edge of heel. Place a ball of stuffing into toes. Sew up row ends of legs, bring markers together at crotch and sew round crotch. Stuff legs, sew up row ends of body and head, and stuff body and head. Pull stitches on a thread tight at top of head and fasten off. To shape neck, take a double piece of black yarn and sew a running stitch round last row of body at neck, sewing in and out of every half stitch. Pull tight, knot yarn and sew ends into neck.

Arms

Sew up straight row ends of arms from fingers to underarm and stuff arms. Leaving armholes open, sew arms to body, sewing top of arms to neck at each side.

Belt

Place belt around waist, oversew row ends at back and sew all edges down.

Shoulder straps

Place shoulder straps over shoulders and sew ends to belt.

Eye piece and features

Place eye piece on head and sew all edges down. Embroider eyes in black, making a chain stitch for each eye and a second chain stitch on top of first.

Backpack

Bring cast-on and cast-off stitches of backpack together and sew up row ends. Stuff backpack and sew up lower edge. Sew backpack to back of Astronaut above belt and to back of head.

Air tube

Sew up row ends of air tube and sew one end to backpack and the other end to left side of body.

Rock Star

Materials

- Any DK (US: light worsted) yarn
  (amounts given are approximate):
  5g yellow (A)
  5g pale pink (B)
  5g grey (C)
  5g white (D)
  10g black (E)
  5g purple (F)
- Oddments of black and red for embroidery
- 1 pair of 3.25mm (UK10:US3) needles and
  a spare needle of the same size
- Knitters' pins and a blunt-ended needle
  for sewing up
- Tweezers (optional)
- Acrylic toy stuffing
- 1 plastic drinking straw
  (³/₁₆in/5mm diameter)
- A red pencil for shading cheeks

Finished size

Rock Star stands 6in (15cm) tall

Tension

26 sts x 34 rows measure 4in (10cm)
square over st-st using 3.25mm needles
and DK yarn before stuffing

Abbreviations

See page 219

How to make Rock Star

SHOES, LEGS, BODY AND HEAD

Make shoes, legs, body and head using A for shoes, B for legs, C for lower body, D for upper body and B for head, as for Skateboarder on page 13.

TROUSERS

First leg

Beg at lower edge using the long tail method and E, cast on 25 sts, RS facing to beg.

Rows 1 to 3: P 2 rows then k 1 row.

Row 4: P7, (p2tog, p1) 4 times, p6 (21 sts).

Rows 5 to 12: Beg with a k row, work 8 rows in st-st.

Rows 13 and 14: Cast off 2 sts at beg of next 2 rows (17 sts).

Break yarn and set aside.

Second leg

Work second leg as for first leg but do not break yarn.

Join legs

Row 15: With RS facing, k across sts of second leg then with the same yarn cont k across sts of first leg (34 sts).

Rows 16 to 18: Beg with a p row, work 3 rows in st-st.

Rows 19 and 20: Work 2 rows in g-st. Cast off pwise.

SLEEVES AND HANDS

Make sleeves and hands using D for sleeves and B for hands, as for Doctor on page 61.

CUFFS

Make cuffs in D, as for Cowboy on page 18.

WAISTCOAT

Using the long tail method and F, cast on 34 sts and work in g-st, RS facing to beg.

Rows 1 to 9: Work 9 rows in g-st, ending with a RS row.

Divide for armholes

Row 10: K6, cast off 3 sts, k15, cast off 3 sts, k5 (28 sts).

Work right front

Row 11: K4, k2tog tbl, turn and work on these 5 sts.
Rows 12 to 14: Work 3 rows in g-st.
Row 15: K2tog, k to end (4 sts).
Rows 16 to 19: Rep rows 12 to 15 once (3 sts).
Rows 20 and 21: Work 2 rows in g-st. Cast off in g-st.

Work back

Row 22: Rejoin yarn to rem sts and k2tog, k12, k2tog tbl, turn and work on these 14 sts.
Rows 23 to 30: Work 8 rows in g-st, ending with a RS row. Cast off in g-st.

Work left front

Row 31: Rejoin yarn to rem sts and k2tog, k4 (5 sts).
Rows 32 to 34: Work 3 rows in g-st.
Row 35: K to last 2 sts, k2tog (4 sts).
Row 36 to 39: Rep rows 32 to 35, once more (3 sts).
Rows 40 and 41: Work 2 rows in g-st. Cast off in g-st.

HAIR AND HAIR PIECE

Make hair in E, as for Groom on page 48.

Hair piece

Using the long tail method and E, cast on 9 sts.
Row 1 (WS): K1, (p1, k1) to end.
Row 2: P1, (k1, p1) to end.
Row 3: As row 1.
Row 4: (k2tog) 4 times, k1 (5 sts).
Row 5: Purl.
Thread yarn through sts on needle, pull tight and secure by threading yarn a second time through sts.

MICROPHONE

Beg at handle using the long tail method and C, cast on 6 sts, WS facing to beg.

Rows 1 to 7: Beg with a p row, work 7 rows in st-st.

Row 8: K1, (m1, k1) to end (11 sts).

Row 9: Purl.

Rows 10 and 11: Work 2 rows in g-st.

Row 12: K2tog, (k1, k2tog) to end (7 sts).

Thread yarn through sts on needle, pull tight and secure by threading yarn a second time through sts.

MAKING UP

Note: Sew up all row-end seams on right side using mattress stitch one stitch in from the edge, unless otherwise stated; a one-stitch seam allowance has been allowed for this.

Shoes, legs, body, head and trousers

Make up shoes, legs, body, head and trousers, as for Skateboarder on page 15.

Sleeves, hands and cuffs

Sew up straight row ends of arms from fingers to underarm and stuff arms using tweezers or tip of scissors. Place cuffs around wrists and oversew row ends. Sew cuffs to wrists all the way round. Leaving armholes open, sew right arm to body, sewing top of arm to second row below neck and hand sloping forwards. Sew left arm to body with hand up in the air.

Features and hair

Work features, as for Skateboarder on page 15. Make up hair, as for Groom on page 51. Sew up row ends of hair piece and sew hair piece to front of hair.

Waistcoat

Sew up shoulder seams of waistcoat and place on doll.

Microphone

Gather round cast-on stitches, pull tight and secure. Cut a piece of drinking straw ½in (13mm) long and place handle of microphone around drinking straw. Oversew row ends of handle along length, enclosing drinking straw inside. Stuff top of microphone using tweezers or tip of scissors and finish sewing up row ends. Sew microphone to front of body and to right hand of Rock Star.

197

Superhero

Materials

- Any DK (US: light worsted) yarn (amounts given are approximate):
  5g red (A)
  10g yellow (B)
  5g pale pink (C)
  10g green (D)
  5g petrol blue (E)
  5g black (F)
- Oddments of black, dark grey, silver grey and orange for embroidery
- 1 pair of 3.25mm (UK10:US3) needles and a spare needle of the same size
- Knitters' pins and a blunt-ended needle for sewing up
- Tweezers (optional)
- Acrylic toy stuffing
- A red pencil for shading cheeks

Finished size

Superhero stands 6in (15cm) tall

Tension

26 sts x 34 rows measure 4in (10cm) square over st-st using 3.25mm needles and DK yarn before stuffing

Abbreviations

See page 219

How to make Superhero

BOOTS, LEGS, BODY AND HEAD

Right leg

Using the long tail method and A for boot, cast on 14 sts.

Place a marker on cast-on edge between the 5th and 6th st of the sts just cast on.

Row 1 (WS): Purl.

Row 2: K2, (m1, k2) to end (20 sts).

Rows 3 to 5: Beg with a p row, work 3 rows in st-st.

Row 6: K2, (k2tog) 6 times, k6 (14 sts).

Row 7: P7, p2tog, p1, p2tog, p2 (12 sts).

Rows 8 to 21: Change to B for leg and work 14 rows in st-st.

Break yarn and set aside.

Left leg

Using the long tail method and A for boot, cast on 14 sts.

Place a marker on cast-on edge between the 9th and 10th st of the sts just cast on.

Row 1 (WS): Purl.

Row 2: K2, (m1, k2) to end (20 sts).

Rows 3 to 5: Beg with a p row, work 3 rows in st-st.

Row 6: K6, (k2tog) 6 times, k2 (14 sts).

Row 7: P2, p2tog, p1, p2tog, p7 (12 sts).

Rows 8 to 21: Change to B for leg and work 14 rows in st-st.

Join legs

Row 22: With RS facing, k across sts of left leg then with the same yarn cont k across sts of right leg (24 sts). Place a marker on first and last st of last row.

Rows 23 to 27: Beg with a p row, work 5 rows in st-st.

Row 28: K5, (m1, k1) 4 times, k7, (m1, k1) 4 times, k4 (32 sts).

Row 29: Purl.

Row 30: K7, (m1, k1) 4 times, k11, (m1, k1) 4 times, k6 (40 sts).

Rows 31 to 37: Beg with a p row, work 7 rows in st-st.

Row 38: K6, cast off 8 sts, k11, cast off 8 sts, k5 (24 sts).

Row 39: Push rem sts together and p 1 row.

Rows 40 and 41: Change to C for head and work 2 rows in st-st.

Row 42: K2, (m1, k4) to last 2 sts, m1, k2 (30 sts).

Rows 43 to 51: Beg with a p row, work 9 rows in st-st.

Row 52: (K2tog, k1) to end (20 sts).

Row 53: Purl.

Row 54: (K2tog) to end (10 sts).

Thread yarn through sts on needle and leave loose.

TRUNKS

Beg at front waist edge using the long tail method and D, cast on 21 sts.

Row 1 (RS): Change to E and k 1 row.

Row 2: P2tog, p to last 2 sts, p2tog (19 sts).

Row 3: K2tog, k to last 2 sts, k2tog (17 sts).

Rows 4 to 10: Rep rows 2 and 3, 3 times more and then row 2 once (3 sts).
Rows 11 and 12: Work 2 rows in st-st.
Row 13: K1, m1, k1, m1, k1 (5 sts).
Row 14 and foll 3 alt rows: Purl.
Row 15: K1, (m1, k1) to end (9 sts).
Row 17: (K1, m1) twice, k5, (m1, k1) twice (13 sts).
Row 19: (K1, m1) twice, k9, (m1, k1) twice (17 sts).
Row 21: (K1, m1) twice, k13, (m1, k1) twice (21 sts).
Row 22: Purl.
Row 23: Change to D and k 1 row. Cast off kwise.

UPPER BOOTS (make 2)
Using the long tail method and A, cast on 14 sts.
Row 1 (WS): Purl.
Row 2: K2, (m1, k1) to last st, k1 (25 sts).
Rows 3 and 4: P 1 row then k 1 row. Cast off kwise.

ARMS AND GLOVES (make 2)
Beg at shoulder using the long tail method and B, cast on 4 sts.
Row 1 (WS): Purl.
Row 2: K1, (m1, k1) to end (7 sts).
Row 3: Purl.
Row 4: K1, m1, k to last st, m1, k1 (9 sts).
Rows 5 to 8: Rep rows 3 and 4 twice (13 sts).

Rows 9 to 15: Beg with a p row, work 7 rows in st-st.
Change to A for glove and dec:
Row 16: K3, (k2tog, k3) twice (11 sts).
Rows 17 to 19: Beg with a p row, work 3 rows in st-st.
Row 20: K2tog, (k1, k2tog) to end (7 sts).
Thread yarn through sts on needle, pull tight and secure by threading yarn a second time through sts.

Glove tops (make 2)
Using the long tail method and A, cast on 15 sts.
Row 1 (RS): (K2tog, k3) to end (12 sts). Cast off pwise.

HAIR AND HAIR PIECE

Make hair in F, as for Groom on page 48. Make hair piece in F, as for Rock Star on page 196.

CLOAK

Using the long tail method and D, cast on 34 sts and work in g-st, RS facing to beg.

Rows 1 to 10: Work 10 rows in g-st.
Row 11: (K2, k2tog) twice, k18, (k2tog, k2) twice (30 sts).
Rows 12 to 16: Work 5 rows in g-st.
Row 17: (K2, k2tog) twice, k14, (k2tog, k2) twice (26 sts).
Rows 18 to 22: Work 5 rows in st-st.
Row 23: (K2, k2tog) twice, k10, (k2tog, k2) twice (22 sts).
Rows 24 to 28: Work 5 rows in st-st.
Row 29: K2, m1, k6, k2tog, k2, k2tog, k6, m1, k2 (22 sts).
Row 30: Knit.
Rows 31 to 35: Rep rows 29 and 30 twice more then row 29 once.
Cast off in g-st.

MAKING UP

Note: Sew up all row-end seams on right side using mattress stitch one stitch in from the edge, unless otherwise stated; a one-stitch seam allowance has been allowed for this.

Boots, legs, body and head

Fold cast-off stitches at shoulders in half and oversew. Sew up row ends of boots and with markers at tips of toes, oversew cast-on stitches; leg seam will be ¼in (6mm) on inside edge of heel. Place a ball of stuffing into toes and sew up row ends of legs. Bring markers together at crotch and sew round crotch. Stuff legs, sew up row ends of body and head, and stuff body and head. Pull stitches on a thread tight at top of head and fasten off. To shape neck, take a double piece of yarn to match body and sew a running stitch round last row of body at neck, sewing in and out of every half stitch. Pull tight, knot yarn and sew ends into neck.

Trunks

Place trunks on doll and sew up row ends at waist. Sew trunks to waist all the way round.

Upper boots

Place upper boots around ankles and sew up row ends. Sew lower edge of upper boots to ankles.

Arms and glove tops

Sew up straight row ends of arms from fingers to underarm and stuff arms using tweezers or tip of scissors. Place glove tops around wrists and sew up row ends. Sew glove tops to wrists all the way round. Leaving armholes open, sew arms to body at each side.

Features and embroidery

Mark position of eyes with two pins on 6th row above neck spacing two knitted stitches apart. Embroider eyes in black (see page 218 for how to begin and fasten off the embroidery invisibly), making a small chain stitch beginning at marked position and ending on row above, and work a second chain stitch on top of first. Embroider mouth in dark grey and make a straight stitch on second row below eyes over three stitches and a shorter stitch below. Shade cheeks with a red pencil. Using silver grey, embroider a star on chest. Using orange, embroider a buckle on waist of trunks, making vertical straight stitches close together at centre front.

Hair and hair piece

Make up hair, as for Groom on page 51. Sew up row ends of hair piece and sew to top of forehead.

Cloak

Place cloak around shoulders and sew cast-off stitches to neck.

Mountaineer

Materials

- Any DK (US: light worsted) yarn (amounts given are approximate):
  5g black (A)
  5g pale pink (B)
  5g white (C)
  5g viridian green (D)
  5g pale brown (E)
  5g brown (F)
  5g cherry red (G)
  2g dark brown (H)
  5g silver grey (I)
  5g dark grey (J)
- Oddments of black and red for embroidery and mustard for making up
- 1 pair of 3.25mm (UK10:US3) needles and a spare needle of the same size
- Knitters' pins and a blunt-ended needle for sewing up
- Tweezers (optional)
- Acrylic toy stuffing
- A chenille stem
- 1 plastic drinking straw (³/₁₆in/5mm diameter)
- A red pencil for shading cheeks

Finished size

Mountaineer stands 7¹/₂in (19cm) tall

Tension

26 sts x 34 rows measure 4in (10cm) square over st-st using 3.25mm needles and DK yarn before stuffing

Abbreviations

See page 219

How to make Mountaineer

BOOTS, LEGS, BODY AND HEAD

Make boots, legs, body and head using A for boots, B for legs, C for lower body, D for upper body and B for head, as for Cowboy on page 17.

TROUSERS

First leg

Beg at lower edge using the long tail method and E, cast on 21 sts, WS facing to beg.

Rows 1 to 9: Beg with a p row, work 9 rows in st-st.

Rows 10 and 11: Cast off 2 sts at beg of next 2 rows (17 sts).

Break yarn and set aside.

Second leg

Work second leg as for first leg but do not break yarn.

Join legs

Row 12: With RS facing, k across sts of second leg then with the same yarn cont k across sts of first leg (34 sts).

Rows 13 to 17: Beg with a p row, work 5 rows in st-st.

Cast off.

BOOT TOPS

Make boot tops in A, as for Prince on page 132.

ARMS AND HANDS

Make arms and hands in B, as for Skateboarder on pages 13 and 14.

JUMPER

Note: Sleeves are worked first and knitted into body.

Sleeves (make 2)

Beg at cuff using the long tail method and D, cast on 12 sts and beg in rib.

Row 1 (WS): (K1, p1) to end.

Row 2: As row 1.

Row 3: P3, (m1, p2) to last st, p1 (16 sts).

Rows 4 to 10: Beg with a k row, work 7 rows in st-st, finishing with a RS row.

Row 11: Cast off 3 sts pwise, p9, cast off rem 3 sts pwise and fasten off (10 sts).

Set aside.

Rep second sleeve as for first sleeve and set aside.

Front and back

Using the long tail method and D, cast on 38 sts and beg in rib.

Row 1 (WS): (K1, p1) to end.

HAIR
Make hair in F, as for Skateboarder on page 14.

BOBBLE HAT
Make bobble hat in G, as for Snowman on page 184.

KNEE PATCHES (make 2)
Using the long tail method and H, cast on 4 sts.
Cast off pwise.

ICE AXE
Head of ice axe
Using the long tail method and I, cast on 3 sts, WS facing to beg.
Row 1 and foll alt row: Purl.
Row 2: K1, m1, k1, m1, k1 (5 sts).
Row 4: K1, m1, k3, m1, k1 (7 sts).
Rows 5 to 11: Beg with a p row, work 7 rows in st-st.
Row 12: K1, k2tog, k1, k2tog, k1 (5 sts).
Row 13: Purl.
Row 14: K1, k3tog, k1 (3 sts).
Thread yarn through sts on needle, pull tight and secure by threading yarn a second time through sts.

Handle
Using the long tail method and J, cast on 6 sts, WS facing to beg.
Rows 1 to 11: Beg with a p row, work 11 rows in st-st.
Cast off.

MAKING UP
Note: Sew up all row-end seams on right side using mattress stitch one stitch in from the edge, unless otherwise stated; a one-stitch seam allowance has been allowed for this.

Boots, legs, body and head
Make up boots, legs, body and head, as for Cowboy on page 19.

Row 2: As row 1.
Rows 3 to 12: Beg with a p row, work 10 rows in st-st, finishing with a RS row.

Divide for armholes
Row 13: P8, cast off 4 sts pwise, p13, cast off 4 sts pwise, p7 (30 sts).

Join sleeves
Row 14: With RS of all pieces facing, k8 from left back, k10 from one sleeve, k14 across front, k10 from other sleeve, k8 from right back (50 sts).
Row 15: P6, (p2tog) twice, p6, (p2tog) twice, p10, (p2tog) twice, p6, (p2tog) twice, p6 (42 sts).

Row 16: K5, (k2tog) twice, k4, (k2tog) twice, k8, (k2tog) twice, k4, (k2tog) twice, k5 (34 sts).
Row 17: Purl.
Row 18: K4, (k2tog) twice, k2, (k2tog) twice, k6, (k2tog) twice, k2, (k2tog) twice, k4 (26 sts).
Row 19: (K1, p1) to end.
Row 20: (K1, p1) to end.
Cast off in 1 x 1 rib.

Pocket
Using the long tail method and D, cast on 4 sts, WS facing to beg.
Rows 1 to 3: Beg with a p row, work 3 rows in st-st.
Cast off pwise.

Trousers

Sew up leg seams of trousers and sew round crotch. Sew up row ends at centre back and place trousers on doll. Sew cast-off stitches of trousers to first row of upper body all the way round and sew cast-on stitches of trousers to top of boots.

Boot tops

Make up boot tops, as for Prince on page 133.

Arms and hands

Make up arms and hands, as for Skateboarder on page 15.

Jumper

Make up jumper, as for Union Jack Doll on page 74. Sew on patch pocket to left side of front of jumper.

Features and hair

Work features and make up hair, as for Skateboarder on page 15.

Bobble hat

Make up bobble hat, as for Snowman on page 185.

Knee patches

Sew knee patches to knees.

Rope and ice axe

Make a twisted cord (see page 218) for rope out of two strands of mustard, beginning with the yarn 90in (200cm) long. Tie a knot 30in (76cm) from folded end and trim ends beyond knot. Thread folded end of rope through a needle and take a large stitch through knitting, coming up at waist. Allow knot to disappear through knitting and be caught in the stuffing. Wind rope twice round waist and sew a small coil of rope securely to left hand. To make ice axe, cut a length of drinking straw 1½in (4cm) long and two lengths of chenille stem each 1½in (4cm) long. Place knitting of head of ice axe around chenille stems and oversew row ends along length, enclosing chenille stems inside. Bend tips of head of ice axe up. To make handle, place knitting of handle around straw and oversew row ends along length, enclosing straw inside. Gather round cast-off stitches at top of handle, pull tight and secure. Sew head of ice axe to handle at centre. Sew ice axe to hand of Mountaineer.

Postman

Materials

- Any DK (US: light worsted) yarn (amounts given are approximate):
  5g black (A)
  5g pale pink (B)
  5g grey (C)
  5g white (D)
  15g royal blue (E)
  5g brown (F)
  5g red (G)
- Oddments of black, red and grey for embroidery
- 1 pair of 3.25mm (UK10:US3) needles and a spare needle of the same size
- Knitters' pins and a blunt-ended needle for sewing up
- Tweezers (optional)
- Acrylic toy stuffing
- A red pencil for shading cheeks

Finished size

Postman stands 6in (15cm) tall

Tension

26 sts x 34 rows measure 4in (10cm) square over st-st using 3.25mm needles and DK yarn before stuffing

Abbreviations

See page 219

How to make Postman

SHOES, LEGS, BODY, HEAD AND TROUSERS

Make shoes, legs, body, head and trousers, using A for shoes, B for legs, C for lower body, D for upper body, B for head, and trousers in E, as for Skateboarder on page 13.

SLEEVES AND HANDS

Make sleeves and hands using D for sleeves and B for hands, as for Doctor on page 61.

HAIR

Make hair in F, as for Skateboarder on page 14.

TIE

Using the long tail method and G, cast on 10 sts.
Cast off pwise.

JACKET

Note: Sleeves are worked first and knitted into body.

Sleeves (make 2)

Beg at cuff using the long tail method and E, cast on 16 sts and beg in g-st, RS facing to beg.
Rows 1 and 2: Work 2 rows in g-st.
Rows 3 to 9: Beg with a k row, work 7 rows in st-st, finishing with a RS row.
Row 10: Cast off 3 sts pwise, p9, cast off rem 3 sts pwise and fasten off (10 sts).
Set aside.
Rep second sleeve as for first sleeve and set aside.

Front and back

Using the long tail method and E, cast on 42 sts and beg in g-st, RS facing to beg.
Rows 1 and 2: Work 2 rows in g-st.
Rows 3 to 10: Beg with a k row, work 8 rows in st-st and k the first 2 and last 2 sts on every p row.
Row 11: *K7, k2tog, k3, k2tog, k7; rep from * once (38 sts).

Divide for armholes

Row 12: K2, p6, cast off 4 sts pwise, p13, cast off 4 sts pwise, p5, k2 (30 sts).

Join sleeves

Row 13: With RS of all pieces facing, k8 from right front, k10 from one sleeve, k14 across back, k10 from other sleeve, k8 from left front (50 sts).

Row 14: K2, p4, (p2tog) twice, p6, (p2tog) twice, p10, (p2tog) twice, p6, (p2tog) twice, p4, k2 (42 sts).
Row 15: K1, p2, k2, (k2tog) twice, k4, (k2tog) twice, k8, (k2tog) twice, k4, (k2tog) twice, k2, p2, k1 (34 sts).
Row 16: K3, p to last 3 sts, k3.
Row 17: K1, p3, (k2tog) twice, k2, (k2tog) twice, k6, (k2tog) twice, k2, (k2tog) twice, p3, k1 (26 sts).
Row 18: K4, p to last 4 sts, k4.

Work collar

Row 19: K1, p to last st, k1.
Row 20: Knit.
Rows 21 and 22: Rep rows 19 and 20 once.
Cast off kwise.

CAP
Make cap using E for cap and A for peak, as for Painter & Decorator on page 30.

POST BAG AND LETTERS
Using the long tail method and G, cast on 14 sts and beg in g-st, RS facing to beg.
Rows 1 and 2: Work 2 rows in g-st.
Rows 3 to 10: Beg with a k row, work 8 rows in st-st.
Rows 11 and 12: Work 2 rows in g-st.
Rows 13 to 20: Beg with a k row, work 8 rows in st-st.
Rows 21 to 23: Work 3 rows in g-st.
Cast off in g-st.

Strap
Using the long tail method and G, cast on 38 sts.
Cast off kwise.

Letters (make 3)
Using the long tail method and D, cast on 8 sts, WS facing to beg.
Rows 1 to 5: Beg with a p row, work 5 rows in st-st.
Rows 6 and 7: Work 2 rows in g-st.
Rows 8 to 13: Beg with a k row, work 6 rows in st-st.
Cast off.

MAKING UP
Note: Sew up all row-end seams on right side using mattress stitch one stitch in from the edge, unless otherwise stated; a one-stitch seam allowance has been allowed for this.

Shoes, legs, body, head, trousers, features and hair
Make up shoes, legs, body, head, trousers, work features and make up hair, as for Skateboarder on page 15.

Sleeves, hands and tie
Make up sleeves, hands and tie as for Doctor on page 63.

Jacket

Sew up sleeve seams of jacket
and sew across under arm.
Place jacket on doll and fold
collar back. Sew jacket together
down front. Embroider three
buttons down jacket in black,
making two small stitches close
together for each button.

Cap

Make up cap, as for Painter
& Decorator on page 31.

Post bag and letters

Bring cast-on and cast-off stitches
of post bag together and sew up row
ends. Sew each end of strap to post
bag. Fold letters along garter stitch
row and stitch together round
outside edge. Using picture as
a guide, embroider lines in grey
on envelopes. Sew a letter to hand
of Postman and place letters inside
bag and place bag on doll.

Techniques

GETTING STARTED

Buying yarn

All the patterns in this book are worked in double knitting (or light worsted in the US). There are many yarns on the market, from natural fibres to acrylic blends. Acrylic yarn is a good choice as it washes without shrinking, but always follow the care instructions on the ball band. Be cautious about using a brushed or mohair type yarn if the toy is intended for a baby or very young child as the fibres can be swallowed.

Safety advice

Some of the toys have small pieces and trimmings, which could present a choking hazard. Make sure that small parts are sewn down securely before giving any of the toys to a baby or young child.

Tension

Tension is not critical when knitting toys if the right yarn and needles are used. All the toys in this book are knitted on 3.25mm (UK10:US3) knitting needles. This should turn out at approximately 26 stitches and 34 rows over 4in (10cm) square. It is advisable, if using more than one colour in the design, to use the same type of yarn as described on the ball band as some yarns are bulkier and will turn out slightly bigger.

Slip knot

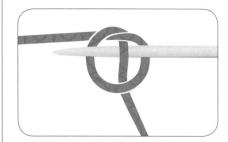

1   Wind the yarn from the ball round your left index finger from front to back and then to front again. Slide the loop from your finger and pull the new loop through from the centre. Place this loop from back to front onto the needle that is in your right hand.

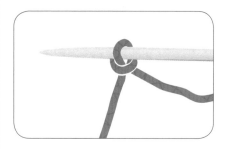

2   Pull the tail of yarn down to tighten the knot slightly and pull the yarn from the ball to form a loose knot.

CASTING ON USING THE LONG TAIL METHOD

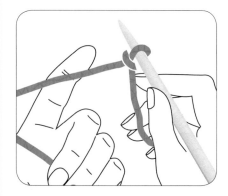

1   Leave a long length of yarn: as a rough guide, allow ⅜in (1cm) for each stitch to be cast on plus an extra length for sewing up. Make a slip knot.

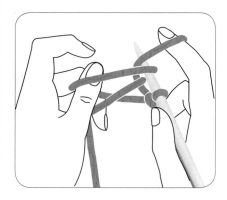

2   Hold the needle in your right hand with your index finger on the slip knot loop to keep it in place. Wrap the loose tail end round your left thumb, from front to back. Push the needle's point through the thumb loop from front to back. Wind the ball end of the yarn round the needle from left to right.

KNITTING STITCHES

Knit stitch

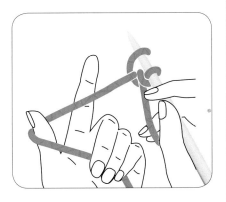

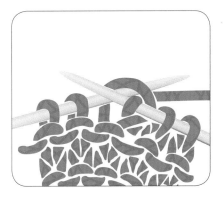

3 Pull the loop through the thumb loop, then remove your thumb. Gently pull the new loop tight using the tail yarn.

Repeat this process until the required number of stitches are on the needle.

1 Hold needle with stitches in left hand. Hold yarn at back of work and insert point of right-hand empty needle into the front loop of the first stitch. Wrap yarn around point of right-hand needle in a clockwise direction using your index finger.

2 With yarn still wrapped around the point, bring the right-hand needle back towards you through the loop of the first stitch. Try to keep the free yarn fairly taut but not too slack or tight.

3 Finally, with the new stitch firmly on the right-hand needle, gently pull the old stitch to the right and off the tip of the left-hand needle. Repeat for all the knit stitches across the row.

Purl stitch

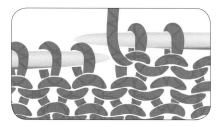

1 Hold needles with stitches in left hand and hold yarn at front of work.

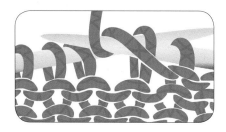

2 Insert point of right-hand empty needle into the front loop of the first stitch. Wrap yarn around point of right-hand needle in an anti-clockwise direction using index finger. Bring yarn back to front of work.

3 Now with yarn still wrapped around point of right-hand needle, bring it back through the stitch. Try to keep free yarn taut but not too slack or tight. Finally, with the new stitch firmly on the right-hand needle, gently pull the old stitch off the tip of the left-hand needle. Repeat for all the purl stitches along the row.

Garter stitch

Stocking stitch

Rib

Double rib

Reverse stocking stitch

Moss stitch

Garter stitch
This is made by knitting every row.

Stocking stitch
Probably the most commonly used stitch in knitting, this is created by knitting on the right side and purling on the wrong side.

Reverse stocking stitch
This is made by purling on the right side and knitting on the wrong side.

Rib
This is made by knitting the first stitch, then bring the yarn between the needles to front of knitting and purling the next stitch. Take the yarn back and continue knitting then purling alternately along row. On the next row, knit all stitches that were purled on the previous row and purl all stitches that were knitted on the previous row.

Double rib
This is the same as rib but two stitches are knitted first, then the yarn bought forward between the needles and two stitches are purled. Continue along row knitting two stitches then purling two stitches to the end. On the next row, knit all stitches that were purled on the previous row and purl all stitches that were knitted on the previous row.

Moss stitch
Knit first stitch then bring yarn forward between the needles and purl next stitch. Continue along row in this way, knitting then purling a stitch alternately. On the next row, knit each stitch that was knitted on the previous row and purl all stitches that were purled on the previous row.

SHAPING

Decreasing

To decrease a stitch, simply knit two stitches together to make one stitch out of the two stitches, or if the instructions say k3tog, then knit three stitches together to make one out of the three stitches.

To achieve a neat appearance to your finished work, this is done as follows:

At the beginning of a knit row and throughout the row, k2tog by knitting two stitches together through the front of the loops (as shown above).

At the end of a knit row, if these are the very last two stitches in the row, then knit together through the back of the loops.

At the beginning of a purl row, if these are the very first stitches in the row, then purl together through the back of the loops. Purl two together along the rest of the row through the front of the loops.

Increasing

Three methods are used in this book for increasing the number of stitches: m1, kfb and pfb.

M1 Make a stitch by picking up the horizontal loop between the needles and placing it onto the left-hand needle. Now knit into the back of it to twist it on a knit row, or purl into the back of it on a purl row.

Kfb Make a stitch on a knit row by knitting into the front then back of the next stitch. To do this, simply knit into the next stitch but do not slip it off. Take the point of the right-hand needle around and knit again into the back of the stitch before removing the loop from the left-hand needle. You now have made two stitches out of one.

Pfb Make a stitch on a purl row by purling into the front then back of the next stitch, by purling into the next stitch but do not remove it from the needle. Take the point of the right-hand needle round and insert it from left to right into the same stitch from the back of this stitch and purl again before removing loop from left-hand needle. You now have made two stitches out of one.

Knitting on stitches

1 Insert the right-hand needle from front to back between the first and second stitches on the left-hand needle and wrap the yarn around the tip of the right-hand needle from back to front.

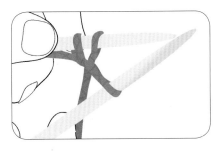

2 Slide the right-hand needle through to the front to catch the new loop of yarn.

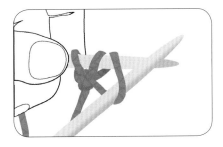

3 Place the new loop of yarn onto the left-hand needle, inserting the left-hand needle from front to back.

Repeat this process until you have the required number of cast-on stitches.

WORKING IN COLOUR

Fair Isle

Fair Isle knitting is used for small areas of colour. It uses the stranding technique, which involves picking up and dropping yarns as they are needed and carrying the non-working yarns along the wrong side of the row. These yarns must be carried loosely to avoid puckering.

1 Start knitting with the main colour (A), which is dropped when you need to change to the second colour (B). To pick up A again, bring A under B and knit again. To pick up B again, drop A and bring B over A and knit again.

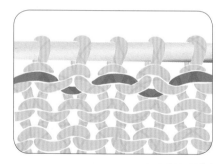

2 On the purl side, the same principle applies: start purling in A and carry B loosely across the back and under A and purl the next stitch. To pick up A again, bring A over B and purl the next stitch.

Intarsia

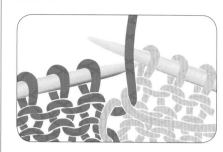

Larger blocks of colour can be worked using the intarsia technique. Twist the two different yarns together at the back of the work with each colour change to prevent holes appearing. Once finished, weave in ends at the back of the work.

SPECIAL INSTRUCTIONS

Threading yarn through stitches

Sometimes the instructions will tell you to 'thread yarn through stitches on needle, pull tight and secure'. To do this, first break the yarn, leaving a long end, and thread a blunt-ended sewing needle with this end. Pass the needle through all the stitches on the knitting needle, slipping each stitch off the knitting needle in turn. Draw the yarn through the stitches. To secure, pass the needle once again through all the stitches in a complete circle and pull tight.

Placing a marker

To place a marker on a stitch, thread a blunt-ended sewing needle with contrast yarn and pass this needle through the stitch on the knitting to be marked. Tie a loose loop with a double knot and trim ends.

CASTING OFF

1 Knit two stitches onto the right-hand needle, then slip the first stitch over the second and let it drop off the needle. One stitch remains on the needle.

2 Knit another stitch so you have two stitches on the right-hand needle again.

Repeat the process until only one stitch is left on the left-hand needle. Break the yarn, thread it through the remaining stitch and pull tight to fasten off.

MAKING-UP INSTRUCTIONS

Mattress stitch

Join row ends by taking small straight stitches back and forth on the right side of work.

Over-sewing

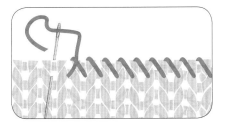

Pieces can also be joined by over-sewing on the wrong side and turning the piece right side out. For smaller pieces or pieces that cannot be turned, oversew on the right side.

Back stitch

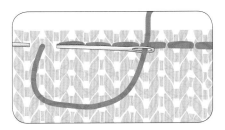

For sewing on hats, hair and belts, sew on the right side of one layer to the layer underneath, and bring the needle out at the beginning of the stitch line, take a straight stitch and bring the needle out slightly further along the stitch line. Insert the needle at the end of the first stitch and bring it out still further along the stitch line. Continue in the same way to create a line of joined stitches.

Running stitch

The necks of the dolls are shaped with a running stitch. Take a double length of yarn and thread a needle and take the needle in and out of every half stitch to create a line of gathering stitches around the neck. Do not secure either end of the yarn but pull both ends tight and knot yarn with a double knot. Then sew ends into neck.

Hem to wrong side

Turn up hem lining and sew cast-on edge to wrong side at the last row of the border, catching each loop of cast-on edge to loop of border. Use matching yarn and work at a loose, even tension to avoid puckering and so the stitches don't show on the right side.

Stuffing and aftercare

Spend a little time stuffing your knitted figure evenly. Acrylic toy stuffing is ideal; use plenty, but not so much that it stretches the knitted fabric so the stuffing can be seen through the stitches. Fill out any base, keeping it flat so the figure will be able to stand upright. Tweezers are useful for stuffing small parts.

Washable filling is recommended for all the stuffed figures so that you can hand-wash them with a non-biological detergent. Do not spin or tumble dry, but gently squeeze the excess water out, arrange the figure into its original shape, and leave it to dry.

FINISHING TOUCHES

Making a twisted cord

1 Cut even strands of yarn to the number and length stated in the pattern and knot each end. Anchor one end: you could tie it to a door handle or a chair, or ask a friend to hold it.

2 Take the other end and twist until it is tightly wound.

3 Hold the centre of the cord, and place the two ends together. Release the centre, so the two halves twist together. Smooth it out and knot the ends together.

Embroidering features

To begin embroidery invisibly, tie a knot in the end of the yarn. Take a large stitch through the work, coming up to begin the embroidery. Allow the knot to disappear through the knitting and be caught in the stuffing.

To fasten off invisibly, sew a few stitches back and forth through the work, inserting the needle where the yarn comes out.

Straight stitch

Come up to start the embroidery at one end of the stitch then go back down at the end of the stitch, coming up in a different place to start the next stitch.

Chain stitch

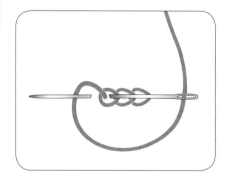

Bring the needle up through your work to start the first stitch and hold down the thread with the left thumb. Insert the needle in the same place and bring the point out a short distance away. Keeping the working thread under the needle point, pull the loop of thread to form a chain.

Back stitch

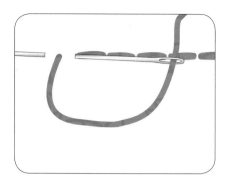

Bring needle out at the beginning of the stitch line, make a small stitch and bring the needle out slightly further along the stitch line. Insert the needle at the end of the first stitch and bring it out still further along the stitch line. Continue in the same way to create a line of joined stitches.

Stem stitch

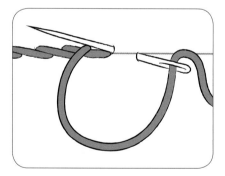

Starting at the left-hand side and working towards the right-hand side, work small stitches backwards along the stitch line with the thread always emerging on the same side of the previous stitch.

ABBREVIATIONS

alt	alternate
beg	beginning
cm	centimetres
cont	continue
dec	decrease/decreasing
DK	double knitting
foll	following
g-st	garter stitch: knit every row
g	grams
inc	increase/increasing
k	knit/knitting
k2tog	knit two stitches together: if these are the very last in the row, then work though back of loops
k3tog	knit three stitches together
kfb	make two stitches out of one: knit into the front then the back of the next stitch
kwise	knitwise
LH	left hand
m1	make one stitch: pick up horizontal loop between the needles and work into the back of it
mm	millimetres
patt	pattern
p	purl
p2tog	purl two stitches together: if these stitches

	are the very first in the row, then work together through back of loops
p3tog	purl three stitches together
pfb	make two stitches out of one: purl into the front then the back of the next stitch
pwise	purlwise
rem	remaining
rep	repeat(ed)
rev st-st	reverse stocking stitch: purl on the right side, knit on the wrong side
RH	right hand
RS	right side
slk	slip one stitch knit ways
slp	slip one stitch purl ways
st(s)	stitch(es)
st-st	stocking stitch: knit on the right side, purl on the wrong side
tbl	through back of loop(s)
tog	together
WS	wrong side
yb	yarn back
yf	yarn forward
yrn	yarn round needle
( )	repeat instructions between brackets as many times as instructed
*	repeat from * as instructed

CONVERSIONS

Knitting needles

UK	Metric	US
14	2mm	0
13	2.25mm	1
12	2.75mm	2
11	3mm	-
10	3.25mm	3
-	3.5mm	4
9	3.75mm	5
8	4mm	6
7	4.5mm	7
6	5mm	8
5	5.5mm	9
4	6mm	10
3	6.5mm	10.5
2	7mm	10.5
1	7.5mm	11
0	8mm	13
000	10mm	15

Yarn weight

UK	US
Double knitting	Light worsted

Terms

UK	US
Anti-clockwise	Counter-clockwise
Cast off	Bind off
Moss stitch	Seed stitch
Stocking stitch	Stockinette stitch
Tension	Gauge
Yarn round needle	Yarn over

About the author

Sarah Keen is passionate about knitting, finding it relaxing and therapeutic. She discovered her love of the craft at a very early age; her mother taught her to knit when she was just four years old and by the age of nine she was making jackets and jumpers.

Sarah now works as a freelance pattern designer and finds calculating rows and stitches challenging but fascinating. She is experienced in designing knitted toys for children and also enjoys writing patterns for charity. This is her eighth book for GMC Publications.

Acknowledgements

The author would like to thank all family and friends
for their support and encouragement during the writing of this book.
Special thanks to Cynthia of Clare Wools (www.clarewools.co.uk) and a huge
thanks to Dominique Page and all the team at GMC Publications.

Index

To order a book, or to request
a catalogue, contact:

GMC Publications Ltd
Castle Place, 166 High Street,
Lewes, East Sussex,
BN7 1XU
United Kingdom
Tel: +44 (0)1273 488005
www.gmcbooks.com